HARBINGERS OF THE APOCALYPSE

HARBINGERS OF THE APOCALYPSE

Poems to Ponder

SANDRA A. HAYNES

Copyright © 2020 by Sandra A. Haynes.

ISBN: Softcover   978-1-6641-3538-3
               eBook   978-1-6641-3537-6

All rights reserved. No part of this book may be reproduced or transmitted in any form or by any means, electronic or mechanical, including photocopying, recording, or by any information storage and retrieval system, without permission in writing from the copyright owner.

Any people depicted in stock imagery provided by Getty Images are models, and such images are being used for illustrative purposes only.
Certain stock imagery © Getty Images.

Print information available on the last page.

Rev. date: 10/19/2020

To order additional copies of this book, contact:
Xlibris
844-714-8691
www.Xlibris.com
Orders@Xlibris.com
820592

CONTENTS

HARBINGERS OF THE TIMES

A Strange Irony	1
Armageddon	2
A Thought to Ponder	3
A Warning Call	5
Apocalypse Ended	6
At the Judgment Seat	7
Calling and Election	8
Closer to Home	9
Covid-19	10
From Here to Eternity	11
God Bless America	12
Harbingers	13
Light Comes	15
Only One Solution	16
Present Truth	17
State of the World	19
"Stay at Home"	20
The Current State	21
The Harvest	22
The Plague of 2020	23
Through the Storm	25

THE BOOK OF DANIEL

A Haunting Dream	29
A Testing Fire	30
Ambassador for God	32
Daniel, God's Witness	34
In the Lions' Den	36
Of Fire and Lions	38
Source of Apocalypse	39
The Chosen	40
The Last Word	41
Weighed in the Balance	42

POEMS FOR MEDITATION

A Closer Look	47
A Friend Indeed	49
A Motley Crew	50
A Searching Question	51
A Sinner's Prayer	52
A Time to Pray	53
Acceptance	54
After Water Comes Fire	55
All about Me	57
All about the Cross	58
All That Matters	59
Angels on Overtime	60
Another Land	61
Answering the Call	62
Assurance	63
At a Loss	64
At Heaven's Gate	65
At His Word	66
At the Crossroads	67
At the End of the Road	69
At Wit's End	70
Babylon, Come Out of My People	71
Be Still	72
Beholding	73
Being Grateful	74
Bread of Life	75
By Every Word	76
Caught in the Web	77
Choices Today	78
Christian Irony	79
Closet Wisdom	80
Coercion	81
Contemplation	82
Contentment	84
Courage	85
Covering of White	86

Crossroads	87
Dark Gethsemane	89
Deception	90
Decisions	91
Default System	92
Drawing Warmth	93
Emmanuel, God with Us	94
Emotional Intelligence	95
Enigma in Flesh	96
Enigmas	97
Enoch	98
Escape to the Light	99
Everlasting Covenant	101
Fallen From Grace	103
Fear Not	104
Fear, a Conquered Foe	105
Food for Thought	106
Force	107
Freedom's Song	108
Fundraising God's Way	109
Garments of Light	110
Gift of the Snake	112
God's Ambassador	113
God's Commandments	115
God's Day	116
God's Judgments	117
God's Love	118
God's Majestic Power	119
God's Man	121
God's Plans	122
God's Precious Promises	123
God's Promises	124
God's Robe of Love	125
God's Sacred Word	126
God's Seventh Day	127
God's Time in Stone	128
God's Unchangeable Word	130
Gods of Wood and Stone	132

Title	Page
Gratitude	133
Heavenly Connection	134
Hidden Nails	135
Hole in the Heart	136
Hope for Today	137
Hosea, Prophet of God	138
Hot Off the Press	140
How Can I Know?	141
In Heavenly Praise	142
How Will You Stand?	143
Impatience	145
In the Garden	146
In the Loop	148
In the Shadow of the Cross	149
Inclusion	150
Inequity	152
Interface	153
Introspection	154
Jesus, Son of God	155
Laodicea 2	156
Laodicea, the Last Church	158
Leadership	159
Light at the End	160
Losing the Lord	161
Loyalty	162
Minutes to Eternity	163
Mary, the Mother	164
Mirror Image	166
No Other Creed	168
Not All Roads	169
Not Just One in Seven	171
Obstacles	172
Ominous State of the World	173
Omnipotent God	175
On Jerusalem's Crest	176
Only Jesus	178
Our Times	179

Pandemonium	180
Parable of the King and His Servants	181
Predestination	183
Pride Goes Before a Fall	184
Rapture	186
Reconciliation	187
Render to Caesar	188
Return to the Cross	189
Salvation 102	190
Samson, a Case in Point	191
Service with a Smile	193
Seven Seals of Revelation	194
Signs of the Times	195
Solid Ground	196
Solutions	197
Star Struck	198
Stewardship	199
Surrender	200
Testing Time	201
Test of Truth	202
The Absence of Time	203
The Big Picture	205
The Death of Reverence	206
The Devil's Tools	208
The Empty Tomb	210
The Force of Love	211
The Forgotten Commandment	212
The Forgotten Day	213
The Gold Standard	216
The Greatest Battle	217
The Greener Grass	219
"The Hound of Heaven" Revisited	221
The Joy of Service	222
The Rainbow Promise	223
The Last Mission	224
The Law, a Test	226
The Rainbow	227

The Man on the Street and Me 228
The Priesthood of All Believers 229
The Principles of Love 231
The Quest 233
The Reckoning 234
The Revelation of Jesus Christ 235
The Seven Churches 236
The Seven Last Plagues 237
The Story of Achan 239
The True Temple 240
The Upward Look 241
The Truth About Miracles 242
The Victory of Grace 244
The Wiser Word 245
"Thou God Seest Me" 246
Touchstone of Truth 247
Travel Companion 249
True Religion 250
Truth 251
True Wisdom 252
Unity in Christ 253
Two Kisses 254
Unity or Uniformity 256
Weapons of Our Warfare 257
What Devil? 258
When Christ Became a Snake 260
When Christ Comes 261
When Crisis Comes 263
When Heaven Begins 264
When Tempted 265
Where Angels Fear to Tread 266
Where Freedom Ends 267
Where Mercy and Justice Kiss 268
Women and Church 269
Wrestling with God 271
Your Identity 272
Your Temple Today 273

REFLECTIONS ON LIFE

A Bird's Eye View	277
A Christian Marriage	278
A Fine Kettle of Fish	279
A Mother's Reflection	280
A Solemn Choice	281
A Tribute to Dad	283
A Woman's Lot	284
A Word in Time	285
A Word to the Wise Woman	286
Action and Reaction	287
Another Anniversary	288
Autumn's Magic	289
By the Sea	290
Carpe Diem	291
Choices	292
Divorce	293
Down the Road	294
Dreams	295
Harmony	296
Endangered Species	297
First Love	298
"Honey"	299
If Gossip Should Strike	300
In Dedication	301
Intimacy	302
Language	303
Masquerade	304
One of a Kind	305
Mother's Model	306
Parenting	307
Political Correctness	309
Power of the Tongue	311
"Rights" vs. Wrong	313
Settle for More	314
Sisters	315
Story Time	316

The Better View 317
The Cost of Love 318
The Death of Modesty 320
The Listening Ear 321
The Missing Piece 322
The Press 323
The Royal Wedding 324
The Single Parent 325
The Snowstorm of 2019 326
Things of Worth 330
Together Forever 331
Tolerance 332
Vantage Point 333
What Every Girl Wants 334
What Men Desire 336
When Calls the Heart 338
White Lies and Others 339
Wisdom 340
Woman's High Role 341
Words 342

CHRISTMAS

A Christmas Treasure 345
Christmas Again 348
God's New Year 350
Irony in the Manger 351
Just Beyond the Manger 352
Message in the Manger 353
Revelation of Christmas 355
Signpost in Bethlehem 357
Special Delivery 359
The Night before Doomsday 360
The Origin of Christmas 362
The Reason for the Season 365
The Week before Christmas 366

Sound of the Drum

God's Spirit will not always strive with the men,
Who dwell on this planet below,
Though God has been patient, the judgment is near,
And the winds are beginning to blow.

As God is withdrawing His Spirit from earth,
It's time to take stock of your life,
To consider your ways, take account of your days,
With the harbingers, vivid and rife.

Tornadoes and ravaging floods take their toll,
While racial disturbance appears,
As evil men carelessly murder and rob,
Increasing men's worries and fears.

Volcanoes erupt, people flee for their lives,
While fires threaten all through the land,
As politics stir up confusion and hate,
Attempting to strategize plans.

Each nation is rattling its sabers for war,
And no one is safe on the street,
Economies suffer as sanctions are placed,
As hope dwindles down at the feet.

Get ready! Get ready! There's no time to lose,
The time of accounting has come,
Then be not complacent and careless today,
Take heed to the sound of the drum.

Dedication

This book is dedicated to the earnest reader who desires a closer walk with God and a better knowledge of His will. In the challenging times of today, may these poems be a blessing to those who read and a reassurance that God is still in control and will care for those who look to Him for guidance.

HARBINGERS OF THE TIMES

A Strange Irony

Covid-19 is the word that's heard on every tongue,
Especially from the ones whose loss, much anguish has been wrung.
We sorrow at the countless numbers growing every day,
With thousands lost in unknown cost of suffering and dismay.

We gasp in sympathy and groan at plague so unexpected,
That took our elders to their deaths while they were unprotected.
Though tragic in its massive scope, the elderly have dreamed,
Have had their families, lived their lives, and played in many schemes.

While all of this is going on, some plagues are undetected,
For what about the thousands lost in efforts misdirected?
I speak of all the infants killed, who never saw the light,
Whose great potential, unforeseen, has vanished out of sight.

Another Michelangelo to us may now be lost,
As victim of the selfishness which spawns this tragic cost.
Another Einstein, wrested from unique and brilliant thought,
May now be slaughtered and unknown, as carelessness is wrought.

A plague is one thing, coming fast, and wholly unexpected,
Abortion is another thing because it's self-directed.
Where is the outcry heard today? Why not on every tongue?
Why not on every newscast heard in anguish duly wrung?

Because of Covid-19's plague, we search to cast the blame,
On those we hold responsible to call them out by name.
And yet, we stand indifferent to those who choose to kill,
The precious children God has made with genius and skill.

Hypocrisy has met its match when we are blind to see,
The devastation which is wrought by this inequity.
We search around with earnestness for cures that may be found,
To stop the current plague with whom our future now is bound.

While all the while, abortion's cure is right before our face,
If we would grasp its value, and its latitude embrace.
For we can choose to stop this plague, as one that we can fight,
And then, perhaps, because of this, the other will take flight.

Armageddon

The chariot wheels are turning; God's judgment soon appears,
Each face is turned to paleness; the heart is seized with fears.
God's Word pronounces warning; His Spirit will not call
On those who have despised Him; on them, His wrath will fall.

The nations now are angry; confusion rules the day,
The time of God's appearing cannot be far away.
For evil men among us will wax the very worse,
Their madness rises wildly, becoming now a curse.

Slaughter of the innocent appears on every side,
The rules of sane convention no longer now abide.
The self becomes the ruler; all others are despised,
The neighbor's interest wanes because of greedy eyes.

Governments vie for power while threats fly thick and fast,
Agreements made between them are destined not to last.
The hope of peace is dying; aggression is the norm,
Protests fill the city streets where angry people swarm.

Get ready for God's coming; the warning is in place,
Though every eye will see Him, not all receive His grace.
It's really up to you, friend, on which side you will stand,
For only the obedient will enter heaven's land.

A Thought to Ponder

As fires now ravage the western coast,
And the air is polluted with smoke,
You're urged to stay indoors so you can avoid
The fumes upon which you might choke.

As people evacuate from the alert
Of warnings by ticker-tape sent,
They flee for their lives and run from the fires,
Which seem upon hell to be bent.

These fires, in the midst of the Covid 19,
Are just the beginning of sorrow,
Which sweep through the land to steal from all men,
The hope of a better tomorrow.

Perhaps it could be for all mankind to see
The folly of life that we know:
The getting and spending, the futile desires,
Decorations, and things meant for show.

The gambling, the politics, fighting to win,
Unrest in the streets of our cities,
The sports that distract us from worshipping God,
Which bring to His heart only pity.

Could it be, we should see that it's time to return
To the God that our fathers once knew,
The God who left heaven to die in our place,
When judgment to all men was due.

It seems we have wandered afar from His will
To travel our own selfish way,
Neglecting commandments He sent for our good,
As waywardness came into play.

We now have approval, our infants to kill,
And genders can marry their own,
Instead of respecting the rules God has made,
Which He to the world has made known.

God said that His Spirit will not always strive
With those who inhabit the earth,
For He will demand an account from each one
To determine all actions and worth.

There's a heaven to win and a hell to be shunned,
It's time to consider your ways,
Turn around and confess that your life God may bless,
As you live out the rest of your days.

A Warning Call

How will you stand in the judgment of God,
For the time is now surely at hand,
For chaos and violence now stalk through each part
Of this once-great republican land.

Our freedoms are vanishing, mischief's afoot
In each open and secretive place,
As Satan aligns all his evil assaults
To bring down our world in disgrace.

Our families are broken apart by divorce
As loyalty fades out of style,
And children, deserted, now roam in the streets,
Engaging in mischief the while.

The highest relation of mother and child
Is forsaken for pleasure and mirth,
While thousands are robbed of the right to their lives
Before they experience birth.

The current religions have turned into clubs,
Ignoring God's sacred commands,
Desiring their pleasures and comfortable ways,
They stray from the heavenly plan.

They banish the worship of God's holy day,
And replace it with one made by men,
Preferring tradition to what God commands,
They cling to the world as a friend.

The people are wary, the prospect is scary,
The honest know not what to do,
As courts enact laws not approved in God's Word
And persecute men who are true.

It's time to return to the truth in God's book,
Long neglected by most in the land,
For only by living the words written there,
The honest in judgment will stand.

Apocalypse Ended

We've waited all our lives for this, and now the time has come:
The final end to which the earth and men will now succumb.
The signs which were predicted by prophets long ago,
Now come in rapid sequence, destruction to bestow.

It isn't like we've never seen calamities before,
But now, instead of far away, they're knocking at the door.
Arriving with rapidity, they pile up on each other,
Not giving breath to catch before there rises yet another.

Hot fires, uncontrollable, burn unsuspecting towns,
Floods encompass homes and lands; desperate people drown.
Tornadoes stalk the land with rage in unexpected places,
They ravage homes within their path, leaving saddened faces.

An unknown virus comes to haunt, sweeping through the nation,
While leaving victims dead in mass and causing degradation.
While all of this is going on, men protest in the street,
As violence and crime increase and peace melts in defeat.

There is no way to look but up as controversy rages,
For all these things have been predicted in the Bible's pages.
For Satan as a roaring lion is seeking to devour,
The earth and its inhabitants, unready for this hour.

It's time to take the Bible out and blow away the dust,
Its Author is the only One in whom to place your trust.
Then let Him be your anchor strong, so with Him you can stand,
Unmoved by all the tragedies that sweep throughout the land.

Be ready for His coming, for it will not be long,
Till Jesus and His angels come to sing with joyful song.
He'll gather all the saints below who look to Him in love,
Who wait for His arrival to live with Him above.

At the Judgment Seat

One day every man will face the judgment seat of God,
For judgment comes to all who ever walked this earthly sod.
The judgment will be based upon the things which you have done,
The life you've lived, the impact made, which speaks to everyone.

The judgment doesn't have to be a scary, dreaded thing,
Although there will be records kept that angels forth will bring.
For men who put their trust in Christ and do the things He asks,
Will find they have an Advocate who carries out the task.

For Christ will be our Advocate; He gave His blood for you,
And all He asks is that you're always striving to be true.
Along with being Advocate, Christ also is our Judge,
Who will not an advantage to His children then begrudge.

He says to cast your care on Him and trust Him to the end,
Knowing He will care for you just as a faithful friend.
He'll meet the devil on His terms and come to your defense,
For He has paid a fearful price, your sins to recompense.

Then go with God and trust His Word and do what He commands,
You'll find that Jesus is the rock on which the Bible stands.
Because the Lord is always true, you need not dread or fear,
Because His judgment favors you, your heart should fill with cheer.

Calling and Election

Hear the heavenly chariots rumbling, restless angels are prepared,
Waiting to receive God's message: Save the people whom I've spared.
All is in confusion earthward; nations rattle sabers sharp,
While in heaven things are stirring, eager angels silence harps.

Those who wait for heaven's glory upward look with lamps all lit,
Waiting for their great deliverance, praying that they will be fit.
Leaders on the earth are baffled, knowing not which way to turn,
Politics with strong division, seek the other side to spurn.

Evil men still roam the cities, seeking trouble that awaits,
Children yet unborn still whisper: Save us from our tragic fates.
Genders, mixed, now wreak confusion, leaving heaven's sacred plan,
Rearranged and now polluted by the fickle thoughts of man.

Heaven's armies, seeking justice, wait in mercy for the few,
Who will answer heaven's calling, dedicating lives anew.
Earthquakes, floods, and fires rage to rob men of their peace,
Thoughtful men by observation sense that problems will increase.

Louder now the chariots rumble; men lack time in which to sleep,
Heaven calls from restless slumber; eternal consequence now creeps.
Open up the dusty Bibles where the truth can still be found,
Wise men, make a sure election on which side you will be found.

Closer to Home

Closer to home, the signs ring out,
Closer to home, there is no doubt,
Closer to home, let's give a shout,
Closer, we're closer to home.

Now let your heart be filled with cheer,
We will find comfort with Jesus near,
Don't let your heart be filled with fear,
Closer, we're closer to home.

Homeless that live on the streets abound,
Trouble on every hand surrounds,
But in our hearts, God's love abounds,
Closer, we're closer to home.

Earthquakes and floods bring anxiety,
Evil men gain notoriety,
Men have forgotten their piety,
Closer, we're closer to home.

People are dying with gun and sword,
Men have forgotten their loving Lord,
Men are determined their wealth to hoard,
Closer, we're closer to home.

Values are lost in the home and school,
Imagined rights have become the rule,
Yet it's impossible God to fool,
Closer, we're closer to home.

Don't let your light now disappear,
Don't let the devil now bring you fear,
Never forget that God is near,
Closer, we're closer to home.

One day the heavens will open wide,
Jesus is coming to claim His bride.
Always and ever to be at His side,
We soon will be safe at home.

Covid-19

Covid-19 stalks about, killing people on its route,
Teens, intent upon their play, try to shrug their fears away.
News reporters, day and night, share the odyssey with fright.
Politicians, doctors, too, are now perplexed, without a clue.

People hold up in their homes, not allowed to leave or roam.
Stocks on Wall Street crash and fall; folks are shaken, one and all.
Parents, home with kids all day, try to supervise their play.
Businesses are shutting down, fearing now in debt to drown.

Doctors scramble for a cure; no one is exactly sure.
How long will the virus last? Despondency, its shadow casts.
Leaders, serious and grave, tend to argue, fight, or rave.
Pestilence now rules the day, stealing peace and joy away.

As God withdraws His Spirit fair, His foe spews poison in the air.
Fires, floods, and earthquakes, too, demonstrate what he will do.
Men have trampled on God's law as prophets all these things foresaw.
Curses, ever long predicted, fall upon the earth, inflicted.

When will men arise and see that they must sin and self now flee?
Violence, greed, and lust are found where unregenerate hearts abound.
Humble hearts are now the need that must for God's own Spirit plead.
Repent before it is too late to find the way to heaven's gate.

Open now the Word of God; make peace with Him upon Earth's sod.
Soon heaven and earth will pass away; will you be ready on that day?
Obedience beckons every man, who will before the Master stand.
The final choice depends on you to seek God's way and know what's true.

From Here to Eternity

"Be wise as serpents and harmless as doves",
Eternity knocks at the door,
When earth's sad cup will be filled up,
And time shall be no more.

The earth's cruel history of striving and greed,
Of tragedy and pain,
Will meet its final reckoning
When God shall come again.

For when has earth such tragic times
And countless hurts endured,
As one by one, disasters reign,
With nothing safe ensured?

And when have men such violence known,
Such disregard of law,
That no one who is living now
Such disrespect foresaw?

Business as usual doesn't apply,
For peace today has flown,
As catastrophes rise everywhere,
With speed before unknown.

Sacred foundations trail in the dust,
Replaced by selfish desire,
While heaven examines accounting books
As time at last expires.

God's Spirit now pleads with every heart
Before it is too late,
To turn the heart from worldly things
To focus on heaven's gate.

Examine yourself, confess your sins,
Be ready God's coming to see,
When each will encounter the coming King
And face eternity.

God Bless America

God, please bless America! If only now He could,
But we have gone our willful way, not doing as we should.
We've left the Christian roots behind which made our nation great,
Hence, chaos, as a consequence, is not up for debate.

We've taken God from every place where He could keep us straight,
We've left no traces of His hand, and trouble is our fate.
What once was wrong is now deemed right, and no one questions why,
For even highest courts agree that infants now may die.

The peaceful protest translates now into a time to loot,
Authority, the villain now, is not allowed to shoot.
Justice hangs her head in shame in hopes that heads may clear,
So we may learn that law is good and not what some may fear.

When handouts in abundance go to not- so- worthy poor,
Then economics takes a dive and hits the bottom floor.
Giving people more than what they'd earn if they should work,
Spawns irresponsibility as their duty then is shirked.

The Ten Commandments were our rock, our guide throughout the land,
But now they're ripped from every place whereon they used to stand.
Insanity now rules the day, as reason trails in dust,
The last thing that we honor now is this: "In God we trust".

As God withdraws His blessing from this once most favored land,
Foundations crumble in the dust; there is no place to stand.
Get right with God, America; your days are numbered now,
When each man, an account will give as all before Him bow.

Harbingers

Harbingers of the Apocalypse rise,
They stalk through this once-favored land,
Where fathers, by spiritual insight were led,
Determined to follow God's plan.

Desiring to leave all the trappings behind,
Of absolute kings and of popes,
They came to this land with courage to stand,
With goals, long established by hope.

With faith in their hearts and axe in their hands,
They carved out a land that was free,
They lived by the Bible, to God only liable,
While forging democracy.

But this noble land was not destined to stand,
For corruption eroded its goals,
Through greed and excess, it has squandered success,
Spawning evil and misery untold.

In time it has fallen away from its roots,
By neglect of God's Word, once revered,
Bringing heartache and grief that can find no relief,
In hopelessness mingled with fear.

As God is withdrawing His Spirit from earth,
Because of rejection of Him,
The god of this world lets his evil unfurl,
Causing hope and desire to grow dim.

Politics stagnate and turn for the worse,
As homelessness often appears,
Children, distracted, can't study at school,
Beset by new worries and fears.

People will argue till unity dies,
Forgetting to fall on their knees.
Nations are angry and threaten to kill,
While gunmen shoot men as they please.

Babies are slaughtered by thousands each day,
As women now powder the face,
And permission is granted for sexes the same,
To marry, despite the disgrace.

When wrong is termed right, it's the devil's delight,
To destroy heaven's image in man,
But God will not tolerate sin on the earth,
And though patient, will soon take a stand.

As earthquakes and fires, volcanoes and floods,
Wreak havoc with force and with power,
Men blame global warming while evil is swarming,
Oblivious to earth's closing hour.

While people are striving, solutions to find,
They hurriedly run to and fro,
Neglecting connection with heaven above,
And the Holy One that they should know.

Though warnings have come, men are still on the run,
Seeking pleasure instead of their God,
It is time to awake and sins to forsake,
With respect to God's measuring rod.

Though harbingers linger, they will not remain,
For Apocalypse comes on the wing,
It's time to return to the truth we have spurned,
As to God all the glory we bring.

Light Comes

Light comes at the end of the tunnel,
Though all may be dark in between,
When trouble surrounds and no light can be found,
Night covers the things that are seen.

But God is still there in the midst of our cares,
For we walk here by faith, not by sight,
And that which would crush all life's pleasures today,
Will banish when cometh the light.

Light comes at the end of the tunnel,
Though hope may be shattered and dim,
Yet all of life's challenges here can be met,
By constant dependence on Him.

For challenges make us the stronger,
When we find God is all we can see,
It is then that we learn to rely on His strength,
By trusting the light we can't see.

Light comes at the end of the tunnel,
For dark only lasts through the night,
The morning will come, though it tarry a while,
And burst into glorious light.

Hold onto God's hand in the darkness,
For night is not destined to last,
God's comforting light will break through the night,
And soon the dark hours will be past.

Only One Solution

We're living in a daunting age when every wind shall blow,
When all around speaks chaos and we face a deadly foe.
As fires, floods, and earthquakes strike, and plague engulfs the land,
There's one thing in God's precious Word that you must understand.

There's only one solution for the frown that's on your face,
For worries that have troubled you, while found in their embrace.
A full, complete surrender to the God who reigns above,
Will give you sweet assurance of His grace and saving love.

If you concern yourself today about your own agenda,
You'll never know the joy of giving up in sweet surrender.
God doesn't want just part of you when giving you a call,
And you will not be satisfied till giving Him your all.

It's only then that you'll be free to let Him make your plans,
For if you've yielded all to Him, you're safe within His hands.
And then, whatever comes to you, He's sure to show the way,
Releasing you from anxious fear and giving peace today.

He says that He will never leave you, nor will He forsake,
If you surrender to His will, your burdens He will take.
A new life He will give to you, new peace and joy to gain,
And in His arms you'll safely rest till Jesus comes again.

Present Truth

For two hundred years, this nation has thrived,
The bastion of truth in this world.
A model to all, sharing that which is good,
Letting light in the darkness unfurl.

The freedom to think, to choose how to live,
To follow the conscience as guide,
These values have fostered a nation that's great,
While being our hope and our pride.

Yet over the years, we have slipped from this place,
We are losing our grip on what's right.
Our Biblical principles, well honored at first,
Have faded in time from our sight.

We tolerate evils we used to condemn,
As forbidden by God in His Word,
And sanction the killing of innocent souls,
As one of our "rights"---how absurd!

We punish the people who stand and protest,
The evils that once we condemned,
We take them to court and ruin their lives,
And make an example of them.

Our greed and our selfishness, violence and drugs,
Now reign as the norm of the day,
Till the vestige of righteousness, killed by consent,
Has slowly been dying away.

We've trampled on heaven's commandments today,
And stripped them of truth that would bless,
While form and traditions have taken their place,
As to men, not to God, we confess.

"My Spirit will not always strive with a man",
Is a warning that heaven made plain,
And as God is withdrawing His Spirit from earth,
Then Satan is given free reign.

Then fires and earthquakes, tornadoes and plague,
The devil then spews on the world.
Killing by thousands the people on earth,
As destruction upon them is hurled.

When men have neglected the Bible as truth,
Choosing as evil, their king,
They can only expect to reap what they've sown,
And must take whatever it brings.

It's high time to turn to the Bible as guide,
Repenting of what has been sown.
To keep the commandments of God's Holy Word,
As intended when first they were known.

Our nation's defection will foster its ruin,
We must break from our wandering today,
And be not a part of the judgment to come,
But turn from the evil away.

State of the World

What can be said of the current times,
When you see what's occurring today?
Lawlessness stalks through our cities and schools
With murder and fear to stay.

Politics vicious will vie for a place
While honesty lags behind,
Movies encourage an evil excess,
With morality hard to find.

Abortion accelerates; children, unborn,
Will never see light of the day,
As mothers dispose of an unwanted child
And carelessly go on their way.

Children are now being taught in the schools
That gender is theirs to decide,
While loyalty both to the country and flag
By some has been set on the side.

Leaders of countries now brag of their right
To destroy other nations around,
While positive news and desirable things
Are difficult here to be found.

Wars and the rumors of wars exist,
As violence with terror survives,
With thousands of innocent children destroyed
Who never will live out their lives.

What can be said of the state of the world?
You can say that it's mostly a mess,
Yet prophets of old predicted this day,
If honesty now will confess.

We're nearing the time when Jesus will come,
Embrace Him, get ready today,
And be not a part of the world as it stands,
It soon will be passing away.

"Stay at Home"

"Stay at home", the warnings came to slow the growing plague,
Yet some, unused to listening, would find the message vague.
Because the plague was far away and not outside their door,
They carried on activities as they had done before.

Because the world had seldom seen a plague as bad and this,
They just assumed that it would be a plague they could resist.
Reluctant to deny themselves until the numbers grew,
They found the plague had spread to them and other folks they knew.

The harbinger of death had come, and they were not prepared,
To face results not then foreseen, if only they had cared.
And when they thought to turn around, they found it was too late,
For many folks would sadly meet an unexpected fate.

The Bible, too, has sent out warnings that a day would come,
In which the world, ignoring God, to evil would succumb.
When men deny the Word of God while prone to self and sin,
God will withdraw His Spirit then and to their choice, give in.

Then Satan pours his toxins out: tornadoes, floods, and fires,
In every tragedy he sends, he spoils the soul's desire.
The wise man who acknowledges and heeds God's warnings clear,
Will recognize His quiet voice and to the Lord draw near.

For evil certainly has come, and each will make a choice,
To heed the warnings given him or thrust away its voice.
Then do not disregard God's Word; His message is for you,
And if God's warnings you will heed, you will be found as true.

The Current State

Some of us are old enough to still remember when,
The world was not so filled with strife, produced by angry men.
It was a time when people worked together for a goal,
And men were hopeful in their hearts of what the future holds.

When patriotism was alive, the flag could bring a tear,
But now it seems the world is filled with fighting and with fear.
Each party in the government insists upon its way,
No compromise arises at the closing of the day.

As racial tensions grow and mount, police are shot and killed,
These issues test equality we should have now instilled.
The media floods the air each day with tragedies anew,
Of senseless, evil happenings that rise to more than few.

The all- convenient gadgets of computer and of phone,
While offering connectedness have left us quite alone.
Our children, small and innocent, are left to choose their gender,
Uncertain as to what or whom they should their trust surrender.

The only hope of earth today, beset with such confusion,
Is to embrace the Son of God and celebrate inclusion.
Yet that will be on God's own terms and not the terms of men,
For He will judge the world with power when He returns again.

The Harvest

When a farmer sows his wheat in the field,
Some tares may also grow,
The tares aren't what he had in mind,
But what he has come to know.

Should he pull them up, or let them stay?
If he pulls them, he may displace
The crop of wheat he's planted there,
He knows that would be the case.

He lets them grow together for now,
For the harvest will come any day,
When he'll gather the wheat from the useless tares
And cast the tares away.

In spiritual terms, the field is the world,
The wheat are the righteous saints,
The tares are those who neglect God's Word
And live without restraint.

The harvest is the end of the world,
When God will judge every man,
He will check the records and give rewards
To those who have followed His plan.

The tares will be burned and turned into ash,
For they have made void God's law,
Though having a choice to do God's will,
They chose from His love to withdraw.

They live together—the wheat and the tares,
The good and the bad of earth,
It isn't until the harvest arrives
That some will be found of worth.

Then let them alone, for only God
Can distinguish the wheat from the tare,
But examine yourself so when harvest arrives,
You aren't found wanting there.

The Plague of 2020

Silently, it came around,
Uninvited, deathward bound.
Wreaking havoc as it went,
On a mission sorely bent.

Gaining entrance to a town,
It ushered in a mournful sound.
Sirens screamed throughout the night,
Bringing people to the site.

Ventilators pumped away,
Adding to the frantic fray.
Medics hurried in and out,
Treating victims on their route.

Working till their strength was gone,
Others came to carry on.
Panic swept throughout the states,
Death to now anticipate.

Sparing no one's creed or race,
The virus moved at fearful pace.
Thousands would to it succumb,
Leaving folks both scared and glum.

People died at such a pace,
Men could not find for them a place.
They loaded them on transport trucks,
Out of space and out of luck.

Running out of rooms to treat,
The leaders would not call defeat.
Instead, more places would be raised
To treat a population, dazed.

Trying then to slow things down,
Rules were made, which brought a frown.
Folks were told to stay at home,
No one was supposed to roam.

Masks were bought to stop the spread,
Some would make their own instead.
Older people were at risk,
Death too soon their lives would whisk.

Teens on beaches had to leave,
While crushing plans, their hearts would grieve.
Students now at home were taught,
As computers, lessons brought.

Overwhelmed by truth unknown,
Men must now their pride disown.
Anchors on the news all day,
Shared the facts and had their say.

Endlessly, or so it seems,
The virus crushed men's work and dreams.
Needing soon their bills to pay,
Some would worry all the day.

A harbinger of things to come,
Men will to these things succumb.
It's time to heed the lesson clear,
That one day time will disappear.

This old earth will pass away,
Welcoming a brand new day.
Just make sure that you prepare
To meet the Savior over there.

Through the Storm

It seems when life is going well, we hardly take the time,
To think about a future life and sacred themes sublime.
It's only when calamity has raised its ugly head,
We rise from our complacency and fill with sudden dread.

We reel with terror at the thought of what may threaten life,
We look for shelter from the storm to hide from fear and strife.
Our thoughts then quickly turn to God when we've no place to go,
We sense somehow that in this time that He's the One to know.

We rush to church, we say our prayers, we hope that God will hear.
Hearts are plagued with troubled thoughts, inspired by nameless fear.
Yet when the devastation slows and life has settled down,
We're then consumed by lesser things, by louder voices drowned.

O fickle man! How slow we are to keep God in our sight,
Until some threatened holocaust has turned our days to night.
Much better would it be for us to stay in close connection,
So when the storms of life appear, we're safe in God's affection.

A daily walk with God involves a time for meditation,
A study of His Holy Word, a prayerful conversation.
For this connection daily sought emits a quiet peace,
A refuge in the storm of life, where fear and worries cease.

Then take the time for God today; He still is in control,
He has a special plan for you; the half has not been told.
Though storms arrive, if you have made of God your special Friend,
He'll be your anchor in the storm when tragedies descend.

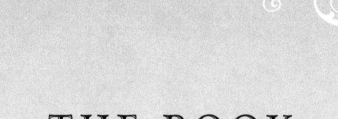

THE BOOK OF DANIEL

A Haunting Dream

Four youthful, Hebrew worthies, captives in a foreign land,
Were witnesses in Babylon, according to God's plan.
One night, King Nebuchadnezzar had a strange and haunting dream,
It came to him from God above, the Ruler most supreme.

On waking, he was anxious, for the dream was on his mind,
He felt it was significant, and the meaning he must find.
It posed a certain problem when he tried to understand,
For the content he could not recall, but felt it must be grand.

He summoned his magicians and the wise men that were there,
Demanding that the dream be told, but they were not prepared.
The wise men then protested, saying none who lived on earth,
Could tell him what the dream contained or what the dream was worth.

In anger, he commanded that the wise men all must die,
For they could not reveal the dream and what it might imply.
Since Daniel and his friends were also wise men for the king,
He asked the king for time so that the answer he might bring.

He gathered up his Hebrew friends since life was on the line,
To plead with God who knows all things, the answer to define.
When God revealed the dream to him, he hastened to the king,
To share with him the meaning, and to God the glory bring.

The dream revealed the future of the kingdoms of the world,
For by the statue in the dream, the future, God unfurled.
In consequence, these Hebrew men were given great applause,
And by them, God was honored, bringing glory to His cause.

We too, must be God's witnesses; He wants to use us all,
To take His love to every man in answer to His call.
God's glory soon will fill the earth, and you can have a part,
By sharing what God wants to do in each and every heart.

A Testing Fire

Three Hebrews face a raging fire
To pacify a king's desire.
He will watch as they are thrown,
To see if God will save His own.

Maddened by their firm rejection
Of his selfish misdirection,
Humbled by their strong objection,
The king in anger stands.

How dare they challenge him this way,
As they refuse to bow and pray?
For is he not the ruler strong,
Commissioned to destroy the wrong?

Honored guests are standing by,
Watching those who him defy.
Power must his role define,
Now that pride is on the line.

Who will save these Hebrews now,
When they refuse their knees to bow?
Flames are raging hotter still,
How dare they boast against his will?

They can't escape, for they are tied,
And by the fire will be tried.
The men assigned to throw them in,
Now feel the flames-- without, within.

The soldiers fall before the fire,
Burned because of raging ire.
All at once, he king now gasps,
Shaken by his vision's grasp.

A fourth man now his eyes can see,
Where once there were but only three.
He forward leans and trembles there,
His eyes, transfixed, can only stare.

The four men stand and walk about,
The fire is helpless, them to rout.
With shaking knees, the king will bend
To three undaunted Hebrew men.

For there, upon earth's humble sod,
Appears the holy Son of God.
The king then calls them out, unscathed,
To honor men whom God has saved.

No rising flood, no raging fire
Can ever quench the Lord's desire.
The men who dare to stand for Him
Cannot be swayed by wrath or whim.

For God has promised to a man,
To honor those who for Him stand.
Then claim His promises, all true,
And He will also honor you.

Ambassador for God

How would you feel if you were a captive,
And brought to a foreign land,
Where few understood the culture you knew,
Or lived by heaven's command?

If you were there with Babylon's king,
And subject to his whim,
Would you be willing to witness for God;
Would you be loyal to Him?

To be chosen by one who was king of the land,
Would imply that one should defer,
To any requests and demands he would make,
And with his suggestions concur.

Would you be willing to risk your neck,
For the things you knew to be true,
When compromise was an easy thing,
Which others seemed willing to do?

If you had been Daniel or one of his friends,
Would you run from the issues at hand,
Or would you depend on the God that you knew,
And search for His Master plan?

It takes some courage and steady resolve,
To swim upstream against power,
Yet God looks for those who will not cave or bend,
But will stand in the trying hour.

Don't wait till the challenge has come to your door,
To resolve in your heart to be true,
But know up ahead, whether living or dead,
That God is depending on you.

You must lift His name as worthy of claim,
Though earth be removed from its place,
For God will then guide you and walk beside you,
While lifting you up by His grace.

Daniel served in a story that carries some glory,
In what he decided to do,
But the question still needs to be answered, my friend,
What if it came to you?

For men are needed who God have heeded,
Who will stand for the right to the end,
For those who have chosen to honor their God,
Have found Him to be a good Friend.

Daniel, God's Witness

I was made well aware of the statute that day,
Announcing the edict that one shouldn't pray,
I was also suspicious that those under me,
Had surely provoked it from sheer jealousy.

I knew that it wasn't the king's own idea,
To instigate laws that might cause one to fear.
He always was trusting and sought my advice;
It wouldn't be like him to plan this device.

I'm also aware that because it's been signed,
If I chose to ignore it, no peace will I find.
I know of the lions; they are hungry all right,
They'd be only too happy to eat me tonight.

The princes are clever, desiring my place,
They are using my faith to bring me disgrace.
Since I've tried to be faithful, no fault could they find,
But now they are working, my future to bind.

It was clever of them, I will have to admit,
But I'm trusting in God to bring glory from it.
It isn't the first time I've had to depend,
On God up in heaven, His angels to send.

I won't try to hide from my usual place,
Of praying to Jesus and asking for grace.
For men need to know that my God's in control,
Perhaps He will use me to save many souls.

My window is open, I'll crank it a notch,
That way, they will see me; I'm sure they will watch.
"Dear Father, you know that this evil is planned,
But whatever the outcome, it rests in Your hand.

If this is Your will, please deliver me now,
Let it be for Your glory to save me somehow.
You've helped me to solve many problems before,
Please strengthen my faith, help me trust in You more."

His prayer now delivered, Daniel went on his way,
To finish the duties he'd planned for that day.
It didn't take long for the princes to tell,
To the king of the trespass, of which they knew well.

The king was distressed at the terrible news,
Though wanting to save him, it was of no use.
Upset with himself for signing the thing,
That night brought no sleep to the unhappy king.

That evening when Daniel was thrown to the beasts,
They gathered around him, from greatest to least.
They roared and they sniffed him while hungry with rage,
While pacing around in the dimly lit cage.

He felt their hot breath on the top of his head,
And wondered by now if he should have been dead.
Daniel cautiously watched as they circled around,
But after some moments, they lay on the ground.

When he saw they were quiet, he knew God was there,
Sending His angels in answer to prayer.
When Daniel relaxed and in peace fell asleep,
He knew that the angels, their vigil would keep.

In the morning he woke to a voice overhead,
Inquiring if he had been saved or was dead.
King Darius then summoned for Daniel's release,
Which made the king joyful and filled him with peace.

The men who had plotted against the king's friend,
Would find no occasion to do it again.
For they and their children and also their wives,
Were thrown to the lions, thus losing their lives.

For God honors those who commit to His way,
No problem gets past Him, no matter the day.
And even if God doesn't choose men to save,
In time He'll reward those who choose to be brave.

In the Lions' Den

When Cyrus had captured great Babylon of old,
And Daniel, the prophet was eighty,
Darius, the king, made him ruler of all,
A title, exalted and weighty.

When the princes he governed were jealous of him,
They looked for a fault to condemn.
They found he was blameless in all he pursued,
Which couldn't be spoken of them.

They wrote up a statute to find him at fault,
Which the king was persuaded to sign,
It concerned the religion that Daniel observed,
Which then would be put on the line.

No man was to ask a petition of gods,
Or of anyone else but the king,
The statute was written to last thirty days,
No petition was Daniel to bring.

The princes knew Daniel would worship his God,
By his window three times of the day,
They knew that he always was faithful and true,
So they waited for him there to pray.

The fine for the man who transgressed the edict,
Was to die in the lions' den,
They hoped that he soon would be meat for the beasts,
It was only a matter of when.

They ran to the king when they saw him bow down,
For Daniel was faithful to pray,
They reminded the king of the edict he'd signed,
Which could not be taken away.

King Darius was sorely displeased with himself,
When observing the trick that was done,
Though he labored to try to deliver his friend,
The edit, its course must run.

Then he ordered that Daniel be thrown to the lions,
Saying, "God will deliver thee."
When he went to the palace, he fasted that night,
Passing the time restlessly.

At the break of the day, he ran to the den,
He called out to Daniel, his friend,
To find out if God had delivered His own,
And if God would His servant defend.

"Oh king, live forever", then Daniel replied,
"For an angel my Father did send;
He has shut the lions' mouth, and I have no hurt",
Hence the king was exuberant then.

Darius instructed that Daniel be raised,
From the den where the animals roared,
The men who accused him were thrown in the den,
Becoming the lions' reward.

The king then decreed that the men of his land,
Should honor the heavenly God,
For He has the power to save whom He will,
He rules on the earth's humble sod.

If you should be summoned to stand up for God,
Remember that God will be near,
For His hand is not shortened that He cannot save,
Nor His ear deaf that He cannot hear.

Of Fire and Lions

What God could not accomplish through the nation that He chose,
He did through faithful servants who did not God's will oppose.
For when they went to Babylon as the captives of the king,
God sent along some faithful ones who would Him honor bring.

He knew He could rely upon these faithful Hebrew men,
Who sought God's highest honor and would not to evil bend.
The Hebrew worthies followed God, regardless of the cost,
Aware that in their perils, they might suffer mortal loss.

Faithfulness in little things had always been a part,
Of what their choice in life had been, enacted from the start.
For even in their daily food, they would not God betray,
They had the deep conviction: they had found a better way.

To bend to men was not a choice their conscience could condone,
They honored one authority: the God upon His throne.
Though people as a whole may fail, God has a chosen few,
Who will to Him show faithfulness, despite what others do.

They witness to the power of God, no matter what the case,
The threat of lions and of fire will not their love erase.
They dare not flinch from peril, but to God are always true,
And if to God you're faithful, He will do the same for you.

Source of Apocalypse

The truth of Apocalypse springs from the books
Of Daniel and John's Revelation.
It dwells on events that occur at the close
Of earth's final consummation.

For man's final end, which transgression will send
Is spelled out in prophecies there,
When humans have filled up their cup to the brim
Of evil, inviting despair.

When men have deserted the truth of God's Word
And allowed it to trail in the dust,
Then evil takes over as substitutes come,
And man forgets heaven and trust.

For nations have risen and fallen through time,
According to God's chosen plan,
The truth is delivered through symbols and signs,
Foretelling the future of man.

As the Spirit of God is removed from the earth,
The devil is given more rein,
Then destruction is seen in the skies and on land,
While causing confusion and pain.

When will man learn the signs to discern,
Which God has revealed in His Word?
For men who will study and seek the Lord's way
Will avoid things profane and absurd.

The warning is given for man to return
To His God, the Creator of all,
That he may be spared from the curse that will rise,
Avoiding his ultimate fall.

The Spirit is leaving and God's heart is grieving,
And mankind will soon reap its fate.
Apocalypse comes with destruction and death,
Change direction before it's too late.

The Chosen

Four Hebrew youth were carried to a foreign land,
As captives of a heathen king, before him thus to stand,
The king saw possibilities in handsome, youthful men,
But these were loyal to a King whose name they would defend.

Though knowing life was on the line in this, a foreign place,
They chose to worship only God, who had their lives embraced.
Determining to honor Him in all that they would do,
They purposed in their hearts while there, all evil to eschew.

It seemed to be a little thing—though it might spell defeat,
Yet they requested simple food, which they had learned to eat.
The rich and lavish food prepared as dainties for the king,
Would only clog their arteries and injury would bring.

They made request of those in charge, who then did hesitate,
For fear the food would cause their health and beauty to abate.
At Last, the eunuch then in charge consented to the plan,
And after ten days passed, he would decide for every man.

In ten days hence, the proof was shown—no others could compare,
With those who ate the healthy foods, for they were not as fair.
And when the king examined them, he found them wiser still,
Than all the wise men in his realm who ate to suit his will.

God used these Hebrew youth to show His power in that land,
Because they honored heaven's truth and followed His command.
And God has promised He will bless the men who choose today,
To put Him first and last and best within their hearts to stay.

The Last Word

The mighty men of earth believe that they are in control,
While overlooking prophecy by messengers of old.
For God will have His say on earth as rulers come and go,
They're subject to His sovereignty, concerning things below.

Like waves upon the restless sea, which lap upon the sand,
They rush upon the shore and then are stayed by His command.
Men rise upon the scenes of earth, intent upon their way,
Yet they are held in tact by Him and kept within His sway.

Great Babylon of ancient time, the wonder of its day,
Once ruled the world, but by God's Word, was destined not to stay.
Then Medo-Persia, Greece, and Rome, as prophesied ahead,
Were ousted in the sands of time, removed by God instead.

The little man who spurns God's Word and rushes on ahead,
Will only reap what he has sown to find ambitions dead.
The church of God-- repressed, unknown, despised by worldly men,
And martyred by God's enemies, will one day rise again.

Though feeble and defective and sometimes led astray,
She is God's chosen citadel of truth for this our day.
She clings to what is in God's Word, tradition set aside,
Though persecuted for the truth, she still is God's own bride.

No earthly power, force, or word can turn God's truth away,
As written in His holy Word for all who live today.
Though kingdoms may assert themselves, yet God will have His say,
When He shall come to reign on earth and all has passed away.

Weighed in the Balance

The wine bubbled red in utensils of gold,
That to Babylon's temple were taken.
They were seized from Jerusalem's temple of God,
Which now had been razed and forsaken.

Belshazzar was reveling in what he had planned:
An orgy of heathen delight.
His eyes were now bleary with women and wine,
Near the end of that desperate night.

As he offered a toast to his heathen gods,
Which were made of metal and stone,
He was startled to see a bloodless hand,
Writing words on the wall all alone.

The reveling crowd was suddenly hushed,
And cowered in obvious fear.
The mysterious writing pricked consciences sore,
For it seemed that judgment was near.

Though written in language that all should have known,
Somehow they could not understand.
They were puzzled and frightened, concerned for their lives,
Right down to the very last man.

Belshazzar then frantically summoned his men,
Yet the symbols eluded them there.
His blasphemous act of abusing God's things,
Was the last straw in which he would err.

The queen knew of Daniel, who often before,
Had interpreted dreams in the past.
He was summoned and given a message from God,
That the kingdom was doomed not to last.

That very same night brought the Persians and Medes,
Who ravished great Babylon's city,
For arrogance summoned destruction that night,
As a scene, devoid of all pity.

Old Babylon stands for the worst in the land,
And its spirit still haunts us today.
For evil and pride with men still abide,
Who are seeking to have their own way.

This spirit again will arise in the end,
When the faithful are summoned to stand,
But deliverance is promised to those who will rise,
To justify God in the land.

Though God may be mocked and derided by men,
They can only take mocking so far,
For God will step in to denounce human sin,
And will have things return as they are.

Proud men seldom learn for they rarely discern,
Till they're weighed in the balance and fall,
But if they will decide in the Lord to abide,
They will find they can then have it all.

POEMS FOR MEDITATION

A Closer Look

Why do we act and behave like we do,
When we know what we do is not right?
Why is harder to put up with folks,
Than to argue, get angry, or fight?

We know that it's better to do the right things,
To say pleasant words which are nice,
Yet something within us defies being good,
We chafe at the Bible's advice.

It's not that we're ignorant, foolish, or dull,
In discerning the man we should be,
But something within us just cannot be tamed,
Though we wish from our vice to be free.

Before Adam's fall, he rejoiced in God's ways;
He knew only that which was good,
But then, when he doubted God's word and he sinned,
God's nature was misunderstood.

Man took on the nature of Satan that day;
His character changed for the worse,
He thought God was keeping some good thing from him;
Self-seeking then made him perverse.

Because of this change, man's words and his acts,
Reflected his inward condition,
Then self- preservation became man's desire,
Which replaced his sinless position.

We think with disdain of a person who kills,
Yet when we inherited sin,
We know not the depths to transgression we'd go,
When provoked by our anger within.

For the Bible says if there is someone you hate,
Then a murderer you have become,
You're no better off than a person who acts,
In anger with senses benumbed.

Societal systems can never improve,
The condition of man in his sin,
For they all overlook the problem of man,
And that which has happened within.

For even religion at times will assume,
That the means justifies in the end,
But when a man hides in religion like this,
His actions God cannot defend.

The heart of a man is deceitful inside,
He will tell himself that he is right,
He will comfort himself by doing some good,
Keeping ugly things out of men's sight.

Yet down in his heart, he knows something's wrong,
What he's lacking is heavenly peace,
Though he laughs everyday as he goes on his way,
Yet his mind will not give him release.

A new birth is needed down deep in the heart,
Superficial solutions will fail,
For only surrender to God's will and way,
In the end will really prevail.

God's Spirit can give inspiration to life,
Transforming man's goals and direction,
Taking the selfishness out of the heart,
While instilling the heaven's perfection.

Although man may turn and surrender to God,
Satan keeps up a strenuous fight,
He'll tempt and he'll try to reclaim what was his,
Attempting to turn man from right.

Man's only salvation and hope in the end,
Is to cling to His Master and Lord,
When he studies the Scriptures and prays every day,
God can keep a man's heart in accord.

A Friend Indeed

Our Father in heaven is partial to you,
You're the apple of His watchful eye.
He salvaged His life and all heaven for you
And prays that you'll choose not to die.

His provisions for you are faithful and true,
His hope as He hung on the cross,
Is that you would respond to His generous love,
So you would avoid being lost.

Nothing else in this life-- no achievement or fame,
Can be more important than this:
To put Jesus first, the Master of all,
The source of true joy and true bliss.

In the morning, turn over your life to His way,
To follow where He may command,
While asking in every decision you make,
To help you to know where to stand.

Committing your life to Him thus every day,
He'll use you to do all His will,
Your talents, your aptitudes, given to Him,
Will He your desires fulfill.

The purest ambitions to which you aspire
If given to His careful hand,
Will bloom and will grow, His blessing to know,
More than you can now understand.

Take time to be holy, be humble and true,
And work for the good of mankind,
Throw self to the wind and put others first,
It's there your true self you will find.

Be sure to establish God's Word every day,
Let His words be your conscience and guide,
You'll find in its message a Friend you can trust,
A God in whose love you'll abide.

A Motley Crew

When Christ chose His ragtag disciples from men,
They had no credentials by which to commend.
They seemed a bit common and lacking finesse,
They resembled a motley crew, I would guess.

But Christ went beyond the rough trappings outside
To discover the hearts where His own could abide.
For He saw in them promise, unbiased by men,
They would rise to the challenge, God's truth to defend.

Though each had his failings, his temper, and pride,
By observing the Master, each fault would subside.
Christ prayed for their growth in His love and His ways,
His prayers were to strengthen them all of their days.

He committed to them special work to defend,
When He left them, their cause with His own had to blend.
They followed the model His life then had set,
Left by examples they would not forget.

Are we not all disciples that Christ wants to use,
Though having our failings which He would not choose?
Then let us surrender, His will to obey,
We can be His disciples and walk in His way.

A Searching Question

"Lord, is it I?" the disciples inquired,
When told one would go astray,
They looked around at every face
For clues to give it away.

The serious words of betrayal would cause
Each man to search his heart,
To see if base deception lurked,
Where loyalty would depart.

The sudden announcement brought panic to each,
They could not imagine the act,
Until the Lord signaled the guilty one,
And betrayal became a fact.

The question still lingers to challenge each mind
Of those who are called by God's name,
To see if some wickedness cherished inside
Might cause a betrayal the same.

If all is not given to God to control,
Then self may rise up and betray,
The Lord whom He's promised to love and adore
When selfishness gets in the way.

Be sure that the heart is surrendered to Him
Whose name you have chosen to bear,
That the question, when asked, can be answered as "No",
When all in the heart has been shared.

A Sinner's Prayer

Lord, help me to never rebel against Thee,
No matter what my inclination may be.
This poor, selfish heart of evil and sin,
Is never disposed to keep self locked within.

Self strives for the mastery, pushing away
The pleadings of Your gentle spirit today.
Create a new spirit down deep in my heart,
And cause inclination for sin to depart.

I'm sinful and hopeless and lost without Thee,
And yet I am longing your servant to be.
Give me love for the souls that are fading away,
Enmeshed in miasma we live in today.

Wash me and cleanse me from inside to out,
Let me see through Your eyes what life is about.
Then help me to keep my eyes fastened on Thee
Until I am all You are hoping I'll be.

A Time to Pray

If ever there was a time to pray,
It surely must be now,
When men are worshipping other gods,
As on the knees, they bow.

The gods of politics and sports
And television, too,
Are promising distractions here
To which their time seems due.

Like Caesar who fiddled as Rome was on fire,
The state of earth we spurn,
Absorbed in things that distract our minds,
We put off God's return.

We pass by the homeless while shaking heads,
Reluctant the problem to meet,
While babies are robbed of life itself,
And thugs shed blood on the street.

Earth's occupants frantically scurry for wealth,
To put in a pocket to horde,
While hardly aware they're becoming a slave,
As money becomes their lord.

Alcohol tickles the throats of men
While tearing their homes apart,
As people struggle for meaning in life
And something to comfort the heart.

While we relish the hope and our comfort in Christ,
The multitudes pass in grief,
Not knowing the value of that which we have,
Unaware of a richer belief.

If ever there was a time to pray
And to work for our neighbors, it's now,
So when the Master returns to earth,
We, along with them, will bow.

Acceptance

Though it's natural to long for acceptance today
So people will think you are nice,
Don't sacrifice values that you should uphold,
That comes at too weighty a price.

Though you may at first be considered as odd,
Don't cave to the need for applause,
In the long run, to stand is much better than praise,
Self respect is a much higher cause.

Though it's hard to stand up for what you believe,
And at times, you may feel all alone,
Yet it's better to stand with your values in hand
Than to waver and have to atone.

If you are consistent in holding the line,
And in other ways, honest and fair,
In time you will gain the respect that is due,
Though some may consider you square.

A battleground isn't a ground for parade,
You're here in the fight of your life,
Yet God will stand by you, the battle to guide,
In spite of the problems and strife.

For others around you, though careless and smug,
Still need to see Jesus in you,
Perhaps you're the person that heaven assigns
To guide them to truth that is new.

Then hold your head high and do what is right,
Be helpful, be thoughtful and true,
For you may be there, the gospel to share,
By doing what Jesus would do.

For Jesus and angels are counting on you
To spread heaven's message around,
If faithful and true to the blest words of God,
Your courage and joy will abound.

After Water Comes Fire

When you have surrendered to Jesus, the King,
And have plunged into waters of death,
You must still be aware of the enemy's wiles,
When rising to take your first breath.

For after the water is sure to come fire,
As the captive of Satan is freed,
Though you find your release has given you peace,
You will find you are greatly in need.

For when you were lost, you offered no cost,
Or challenge to Satan, the foe,
But now that you're free from his sophistry,
He has weapons of which you don't know.

When you think you can rest from temptation with ease,
And can finally let down your guard,
He still has some tricks that he keeps up his sleeve,
Which he plays with reckless regard.

He will cause you to feel since you've publicly shown,
That you now are a child of the King,
That there's no need to study and pray every day,
For it seems but a trivial thing.

He also will tempt you to feel that you're strong,
Forgetting the weakness of flesh,
He will tempt you to wander in previous paths,
While wounding the Master afresh.

And if you should happen to stumble and fall,
He will cause you to wallow in shame,
Afraid that because you have fallen away,
You can't heaven's mercy reclaim.

He studies you closely and knows where you're weak,
He will cause you to doubt heaven's worth,
And to think it is foolish to live for the Lord,
While you spend your time here on the earth.

Though Satan is present to tempt and confuse,
God's angels are mighty in power,
They will give you the strength to keep up your guard,
And resist Satan's wiles every hour.

The only escape is to stay with the Lord,
By prayer and constant devotion,
Only then will you find you may have peace of mind,
As you drink of the heavenly potion.

All about Me

"It's all about me", and it's not hard to see
That the world has accepted the theme,
It started in heaven when evil like leaven
Was spawned by a devilish scheme.

Since then, it has grown, for men tend to own
Its self-centered emphasis now.
Get all that you can is the obvious plan,
Which has won the world over somehow.

You see it in politics, commerce, and homes,
When self rises high on the throne,
When others are treated as less than oneself,
It can cause them to suffer and moan.

The spirit of Satan invades to the point
Where a woman will kill her own child,
For "It's all about me" is all she can see,
When she used to be thoughtful and mild.

It's natural to grasp everything that one sees,
For man has departed from grace,
But God has a plan to restore every man,
So that we may His image embrace.

For the spirit of heaven is not on itself,
It's focused on serving another,
While made in God's image, we must copy Him,
By helping our sisters and brothers.

Our happiness centers in being like God,
For His thoughts are higher than ours,
If we waste our lives thinking only of self,
We will then be destroying our powers.

If you hope to do good in this life as you should,
Just forget that "It's all about me",
You'll find that in caring for others, my friend,
You're creating your own destiny.

All about the Cross

It's all about the cross; there's just no other way,
The cross requires some suffering: there is a price to pay.
The servant is not greater than the Lord who paid the price.
There is no crown or heavenly prize without a sacrifice.

Though Jesus paid the wages for each soul to be like Him,
Our characters must be refined to join with seraphim.
Our trials and afflictions here will work out all the dross,
So we may hope to be like Him while carrying our cross.

All pride and self-sufficiency must be surrendered now,
All talents that He's given us must here before Him bow.
The willingness to take His name when others criticize,
Is such a meager price to pay when heaven is the prize.

Such inspiration comes from His great suffering and His pain,
His willingness to die for us that we might heaven gain.
His patience and His tender care while dying on the cross,
Persuades us heaven's cheap enough, whatever be the cost.

All That Matters

When comes your final day on earth, what good will you have done?
Will things you have accomplished here bring joy at closing sun?
For houses, clothes, and pedigrees will insignificant be,
If you have not humanity blessed in all sincerity.

The only thing of value then is what you've done for others:
The needy folks whom you may meet—your sisters and your brothers.
A caring smile, a helpful hand, a willing ear to listen,
Are things the world is craving now—to wipe the tears that glisten.

Education and wealth are fine if used to help where needs abound,
But when they're used to gratify self, they're seldom useful found.
For all of heaven is now astir in ministering to others,
The only joy in life is found in knowing you've helped a brother.

Then open your heart to listen well to others along the way,
It just may be, by doing so, that you will make their day.
Be slow to speak, yet quick to hear of burdens they may bear,
You'll find that you will both be blessed by showing that you care.

Angels on Overtime

God sends His mighty angel staff to care for you each day,
He watches lest you slip and fall to help you when you stray.
Though God has sent His angels strong from heaven's realm sublime,
Don't be presumptuous, making angels work on overtime.

When thinking you can charge ahead and push the envelope,
You may discover in the end, you're on a slippery slope.
God's promises to keep you safe deserve cooperation,
Presumption comes with penalties that may have long duration.

To put oneself at risk is never safe nor is it wise,
Lest walking into danger, one is startled by surprise.
Whether you are taking risks of body or of soul,
Don't work your angel overtime by actions that are bold.

Salvation is a costly thing; it came with heavy price,
Because it was the precious blood of Jesus' sacrifice.
Accept God's gift with gratitude and treasure it as prime,
Lest you be charged with making angels work on overtime.

Another Land

Eye hath not seen, ear hath not heard,
Neither have entered man's heart,
The things which God is preparing for him,
Decided in love from the start.

For earth is a cauldron of futile desires,
Which seldom finds wings and can fly.
It's only as we to the Scriptures refer,
That hope blooms on which to rely.

Though moments arise to be treasured on earth,
They mingle with loss and with pain,
For sickness and tragedy darken our dreams
And cause us to question our gain.

But there is a place to which we may go,
Unfettered by tears or by loss,
Its price has been paid by a plan that was made,
Involving some nails and a cross.

To those who are faithful, it comes as a gift,
With a new name upon a white stone,
To those who have treasured the high sacrifice
That was given by Jesus alone.

No eye can imagine the furnishings there,
The beauty and peace that abide,
The rapture of hearing the angels' songs,
With Jesus and friends by one's side.

No tears or death will inhabit that place,
No mourning or sighs will abound,
The freshness of morning will bring only joy
As the birds warble glorious sound.

There's a heaven to win and a hell to shun
And a Father who waits above,
To welcome His wandering children at last,
Encircling them with His love.

Answering the Call

Are you tuned in to the Spirit? Does He have your ear today?
Will you know if you are summoned when a need comes into play?
Will you give a ready answer, or be too busy then?
When a person needs assistance, will you be a faithful friend?

If you haven't had much practice, listening for the Spirit's voice,
Will you then be quick to answer when He brings to you a choice?
Is your heart to heaven open? Have you heard God's voice before?
Or will the voice that speaks to you be somehow just ignored?

You must keep the channel open so you quickly can respond,
To the needs that are around you and the needs that lie beyond.
You can be the Savior's helper and in readiness stand by,
You can bring a new assurance to the ones about to die.

When you pray and listen closely, you will hear the Spirit speak,
He will teach you how to help another with His own technique.
If you let the Spirit use you, you will find that in the end,
It will bring you joy unending and perhaps a grateful friend.

Assurance

Because we hail from Adam's stock, there's something that we lack,
When things don't happen fast enough, somehow we will react.
We find we lack the patience just to sit around and wait,
For things we asked for long ago and still anticipate.

Where are you, God? Are You still there? And don't You understand?
For waiting and uncertainty were never in my plan.
Yet pain and trouble came my way and family problems, too,
I am bereft, for what is left? I don't know what to do.

I know You have the answers, Lord; Your book has told me so,
Your providence is hid from me; it's not for me to know.
Your people languish in this world with equity amiss,
They cling to hope and promises of happiness and bliss.

We grope in shadows of this life and look for comfort here,
Yet comfort has eluded us; we wrestle with our fear.
Oh, God of Job and Jacob, too, they wrestled with you then,
And pleaded for deliverance, which only You could send.

Because You heard their plaintive cry, I know You'll hear me, too,
And though I may not hear Your voice, I know just what to do.
For I have found Your faithfulness is all I'll ever need,
And that Your words are bread enough on which my soul can feed.

At a Loss

What can you say to a person today
Who has lost his dearest friend,
When somehow, words can't sense or know
The needed message to send?

It's a time when silence is golden, my friend,
And when that which is easy to hear,
Is the message that hearts are together alone,
Lacking words that may deafen the ear.

The one who is facing the loss is aware
That you cannot perceive what he feels,
Relating to death is intrinsic to each,
Which often is never revealed.

The best he can know is your presence is there,
Providing just what he may need,
Your interest in what he is facing today
Will offer him comfort indeed.

Abundance of words is not helpful right now,
His mind is already a blur.
Let him speak whenever he's able to speak,
Let things in a calm way occur.

When the dust has finally settled at last,
And he's coming to grips with the thing,
You will find that your bonds are stronger for this,
Which comfort to both will then bring.

At Heaven's Gate

How could heaven be heaven, my friend,
If you're missing at heaven's gate?
For someone will miss you, whoever you are,
That fact is not up for debate.

The Father loves you like no one else could,
He loved you before you were born.
He made you especially to be just like Him,
Be ready to meet Him that morn.

A kindly affection bonds hearts that connect,
You are special to those you know.
It's only the devil who wants you to think
You don't matter on earth below.

God has given you talents to share with the world,
Each person is truly unique.
He's made a position in which you can shine,
If you will His confidence seek.

Though no one is perfect, and each has his faults,
God promised He'd turn you around.
He can change your direction and give you new goals,
And you can be heavenward bound.

God forever will miss those who turn from His love,
For you He has given His all,
And heaven will be so much sweeter for Him,
If you will respond to His call

At His Word

Is the Lord particular? Let's ask our mother Eve,
Who brought on earth more problems than any could conceive.
And what about her firstborn son who lived in times of old,
Who disregarded God's command and killed his brother cold?

In Noah's time God warned the folks to climb into the ark,
Yet all but eight would meet their fate, refusing to embark.
Consider Father Abraham, whose faith at times was weak,
Who ran ahead of God's own plan, the promised son to seek.

Is the Lord particular? I'm thinking of a fish,
Who swallowed the prophet Jonah while spurning heaven's wish.
When God's great leader, Moses, disregarded the Lord's command,
He lost his chance by striking the rock and missed the promised land.

Many other examples remain of folks who disobeyed,
Who found that all too late in life, a price for sin is paid.
We needn't try to tempt the Lord or try to circumvent
Instructions given for our good, which He has kindly sent.

But take God's Word and cherish it and let it be your guide,
You'll find in Him a faithful Friend, in whom you can confide.
Because He means just what He says, you'll find His Word is true,
And if you choose to follow it, much joy will come to you.

At the Crossroads

As a nation, we claim we are Christians,
Yet now it's OK to be gay,
Though the Bible is very specific
That this habit will lead one astray.

What used to be wrong is called right,
Folks are criticized if they protest,
And people may call it a hate crime,
Which might even spawn an arrest.

The issue of rights now has blossomed,
And it seems it will not be restrained,
Though the Bible has always placed limits and rules
To keep certain evils contained.

We now destroy infants in slaughter,
When we used to guard innocent life,
No wonder the cities are reeling today
With infamy, killing, and strife.

The things that we used to hold sacred,
Protecting with reverence and awe,
Are carelessly being polluted today,
For we have made void heaven's law.

We wonder at nature's upheaval today,
At floods, hurricanes, and the like,
At weather that's wreaking great havoc,
When taking a notion to strike.

God said if His erring creation,
The ones who are called by His name,
Will turn from their sins in repentance,
He will heal and love them the same.

If not, He has promised destruction
For those who refuse to repent,
The ones who deny heaven's counsel,
And are firmly on evil now bent.

It's time to take stock of our actions,
Decisions so poorly contrived,
Reclaiming our once-noble country,
Where values once peacefully thrived.

Rebuking the evil among us
And standing for that which is right,
Will give us a new direction today
As we follow the God-ordained light.

At the End of the Road

Heaven is closer to those in God
Who have fallen in death asleep,
Than for those of us who here remain,
Being left for their loss to weep.

Though they sleep for a day or many years,
The next thing the dead will hear,
Will be the call from their dusty grave
When the Savior will appear.

They rest in peace in the Father's love,
Their trials all laid aside,
Having fought the fight of living faith,
They are waiting to be His bride.

The enemy cannot tempt them now,
They are safe in the Master's hand.
They await the resurrection day
From this dark and dreary land.

The choice awaits each one who lives,
And what will your answer be?
Will you choose this world of limited bliss,
Or opt for eternity?

To put off the choice means you already have
Decided to follow the world,
You have chosen the selfish, wayward path
While rejecting the heavenly pearl.

Though this world may seem to offer you light,
In the end, it will all be dark,
Be careful of the choices you make
And the plans on which you embark.

For the grave cannot hold the souls of those
Who focus on heaven above,
They will rise at the second coming of Christ,
To be wrapped in eternity's love.

At Wit's End

When you're at your wit's end and in need of a friend,
Just remember that Jesus is there,
At the end of your rope, there is reason for hope,
For He's promised to comfort and care.

When the world does you in with its troubles and sin,
The solution is found in God's Word,
For His message to you with its answers are true,
You will find they're the best ever heard.

Don't get lost in the maze of these troublesome days,
But rely on the God who is true,
He won't let you down; He'll remove anxious frowns,
For His love and His joys are for you.

Just tell Him your problems and give Him your cares,
For He has a plan for your life,
He will open the way to enlighten your day
And relieve you from care and from strife.

Babylon, Come Out of My People

God's people are not Babylon, though some have called them so,
Yet sometimes in a Christian's heart, old Babylon's ways may show.
The inclination of Babylon, which began with the Tower of Babel,
Is to try to work one's way to God to prove that one is able.

For instance, the city of Babylon of Nebuchadnezzar the great,
Was built on man's presumptive pride, which finally caused its fate.
When Nebuchadnezzar began to brag, in glory to self alone,
God caused this king to graze in the field, deposing him from his throne.

In the center of false religions lies the desire to save oneself,
Forgetting the price was already paid by heaven's costly wealth.
The final end of Babylon's fate is prophesied as hell,
Along with all who share this view that works will prove them well.

No mantras of repeated words, no penance on one's knees,
No flagellation of the back will heaven's God appease.
The only gift that man can bring to satisfy the King,
Is humble, willing obedience to God's requested thing.

An eagerness to obey God's Word and the law on which He stands,
Is found in a heart of gratitude that follows His commands.
Good works will follow surrender, but not to erase mistakes,
But rather from a grateful heart, which of God's love partakes.

Then God can take the willing heart and make it like His own,
No useless beating of the air can whisk one to His throne.
But in the sweet surrender of all a person may be,
The man will find God's highest joy, fulfilling his destiny.

Be Still

In our fast and frantic pace of life, God calls us to be still,
So we may find the path of life by learning of His will.
The steady noise and stressful thoughts that plague our every day,
Distract from focusing on Him, and thus we lose our way.

The quiet moments must be found to open up God's Word,
Wherein its sacred passages, His voice can still be heard.
The longing in the heart of man for what will gratify,
Is often sought through earthly things that cannot satisfy.

The only peace that can be found is in the sacred page,
Where God can speak to every heart, surrender to engage.
Life's pressing cares and challenges will softly fade away,
As hope and grace envelop them to keep life's trials at bay.

New strength and hope will take the place of what has plagued the mind,
And in this close encounter, man will there an anchor find.
Then choose a time to spend with God; be still, His voice to hear,
You'll find the time has been well-spent in banishing your fear.

Beholding

We're changed as we embrace the things we often choose to view,
This is a proven principle affecting me and you.
We're made to be reflectors of the character of God,
Observing Him, we'll be a blessing on this earthly sod.

The tree in the Garden of Eden above was an opportunity rare,
For Eve to prove her devotion and to live for eternity there.
Instead of her reflecting God, she wanted to be the Light,
Which is a form of idolatry, which created earth's dark night.

Because we're made to be like God, He wants us to shine for Him.
By choosing ourselves to worship, it makes our light grow dim.
For man can never rise above the thing which he may cherish,
If self becomes the focus, he sooner or later will perish.

The creature is not greater than the God who has made him so,
And man's attempt to challenge His God is not the way to go.
Our reasoning is idolatry if chosen over God's,
There is no way if we should stray that we can beat the odds.

We often tend to copy the things which we may idolize,
And we will rise no higher than the things which we may prize.
It's always better to trust in God, reflecting His love and worth,
So we can fill the role which God has planned for us at birth.

Being Grateful

What does it mean to be grateful?
Is it only a nod of the head,
When you are preparing to eat your food,
Or climbing into your bed?

It seems to me to be grateful
Is more about how you live,
In showing appreciation to God,
By what you're willing to give.

To give an offering is helpful,
When put in the offering plate,
But what will you do in the meantime
When others are hungry and wait?

For if you are thankful for what you possess,
You will want to share with another,
For even the man who lives on the street
By creation is your brother.

For even Christ in His glory above
Was willing to leave all behind,
To descend from heaven's abundance,
The weary and helpless to find.

Then if you are truly grateful, dear friend,
There's a world out there in need,
You can show your appreciation today
By doing a kindly deed.

Bread of Life

Nourishment hides in the Bread of life,
For man is a spiritual soul,
He depends on the message in God's living Word
To make him complete as a whole.

Men take a great interest in physical food
And relish the joy that it gives,
Yet they will forget that the food of God's Word
Will teach a man how he should live.

For what is a body that's lacking the food
That offers perspective on life,
That guides man to value the things of worth,
To steer him from hatred and strife?

When reading God's Word, there's a Spirit within
That changes and softens the heart,
That quickens and strengthens a holy resolve
To teach one from sin to depart.

God's law is a transcript of all that He is,
You'll find Jesus Christ deep inside,
And if you will eat of the nourishment there,
His truth with you then will abide.

A man wouldn't think of not eating each day,
Or eating just once in a week,
And yet he will skip many days without God,
Forgetting to nourishment seek.

When eating God's Word, we are eating His flesh,
And thus, we become more like Him,
For Christ is the essence of all it contains,
He's promised to fill to the brim.

Then feast every day on His glorious Word,
His message is written for you,
The nourishment you will receive from His Word
Will keep you both faithful and true.

By Every Word

On Friday, Christ was crucified; on Saturday, He rested,
The Sabbath was established long before it was contested.
Before a Jew was ever born, God's day was set in place,
Because it was intended for all men within the race.

Christ kept the Sabbath in His life and even in His death,
For at the first He issued it with His own sacred breath.
For He is God, He changes not; you cannot change perfection,
Yet man has tried to change God's law by his own false perception.

The seventh day is here to stay; you'll find it's kept in heaven,
For only Sabbath has been blessed, not number one, but seven.
There is no change within God's Word to worship on the first,
Though men's traditions for this day are often still rehearsed.

It's better not to follow men, for they are often wrong,
The Bible is the test of truth; its words are sharp and strong.
We dare not try to pick and choose the message it should say,
So we can suit our preferences and wipe God's words away.

Then set your feet in heaven's path and worship on God's day,
A blessing lies within its hours that will not pass away.
For every seventh day in time, the faithful there will meet,
To worship Jesus, King of kings, while sitting at His feet.

Caught in the Web

Have you ever once stolen a thing that you craved?
If you have, you will never forget,
The rush of excitement that comes with the quest,
Then followed by sinking regret.

Whatever the thing you desired to obtain,
To claim as a thing you might own,
The pleasure is haunted by riddling guilt,
Which selfishness likely has sown.

Whether you're found out or whether you're not,
You still will be robbed of your peace,
For when it's all over and quietness comes,
Your conscience will seek for release.

No matter what we as a people may have,
We tend to desire something more.
New things seem much better than what we possess,
Whether we're rich or we're poor.

The only solution for such a desire,
Is to value the things that you own,
And look not to others and what they may have,
Lest sordid seeds then may be sown.

When you have determined inside to be true,
You also to others will be,
Then you won't be caught in the coveting web,
As a matter of honesty.

Choices Today

There are things that can trouble the thoughtful mind:
The abuse of children and beasts,
The illegal traffic of women and youth,
The rejection of those who are least.

The reckless abandon of murderous fiends,
The greedy ambitions of men,
The constant resistance to humble oneself,
To make of the foe a new friend.

The granting of freedom to disregard laws,
As spoken in God's Holy Word,
Allowing the murder of innocent blood,
While sanctioning actions absurd.

Just where we are headed is easy to see,
Casting caution aside isn't new,
But there is a price that will have to be paid,
Determined by what we will do.

God's Word gives the pattern of actions to take,
For nations to grow and succeed,
Its laws are in place to insure to each race,
Their compliance will meet every need.

When nations have ventured to step out of line,
With the pattern that God put in place,
You can then be assured that destruction will come,
For defying the Lord to His face.

For vengeance is His, though for Him, it is strange,
Yet there's only one answer for peace.
God has set it in place for the whole human race,
When it's followed, then conflict will cease.

Then consider your ways for the rest of your days,
Don't be caught in the trap of defeat,
For another world beckons that offers much more,
Where the righteous will sit at God's feet.

Christian Irony

Though we be poor, yet are we rich and blessed with peace above,
Although we suffer hate and scorn, we bask in heaven's love.
Though sorrowful, we still rejoice, forgotten, yet well-known,
Bereft, yet not despondent, with warmth from coldness shown.

For neither stripes, imprisonment, or any other thing,
Can steal from us the glory that the Lord in time will bring.
The light affliction that we know, we cannot now compare,
With all the joys that wait for us in heaven's glory there.

For though we sigh and struggle here, new life springs from within,
We're strengthened by God's mighty arm, another soul to win.
Though bothered by a tempest strong, anxiety will cease,
Held safely in the Master's arms, we rest in quiet peace.

Closet Wisdom

Some things should remain in the closet,
In fact, they should never exist.
In this day of unbridled indulgence,
Iniquity grows and persists.

Things that are seen as a "right" by men,
By God are considered as wrong,
And no legislation by humans today
Can fix them so that they belong.

Because of equality issues today,
Men mix what is right with what's wrong.
They clamor for things once forbidden,
Which grow until wayward and strong.

The issues then foster confusion
As they stray from God's practical plan,
The result is not healthy or helpful
But creates a degenerate man.

When society chooses to wander,
To leave truth as found in God's Word,
The result is always disaster,
Encouraging what is absurd.

The only safe pathway to follow,
If one would be healthy and whole,
Is to walk in the pathway of Jesus,
Who alone can give life to the soul.

Coercion

Any religion that needs to use force
Cannot be religion that's true.
Jesus died on the cross at infinite cost
To offer His freedom to you.

The option to worship the God that you choose,
Not one who coerces by force,
Produces cooperation and love
Because of its generous source.

God gives every man the option to stand
With a force that stands as true,
He also gives freedom for man to do wrong,
Though penalties often come due.

For choice is important; when men are oppressed,
Creativity dies on the vine,
For love is a thing that cannot be forced,
For love is a thing that's divine.

Be generous, friend, for God in the end
Will judge every man by his acts,
For conscience alone must each person persuade,
Remaining a Biblical fact.

Then let a man choose and do not abuse
The right God has given to all,
And perhaps it may be that heaven you'll see,
When God comes to finally call.

Contemplation

What do you do when you've failed to act
On the values that you hold?
Do you beat yourself up and wallow in guilt
For falling out of God's mold?

Do you feel embarrassed to face yourself,
Though others may not be unaware?
Do you spend your time with a guilty heart,
Do you mope around and stare?

You must first confess your failure to act
In the way you thought you should.
You must ask forgiveness of God and self,
Regaining ground where you stood.

You must look at motives that made you act,
Understanding why you have failed.
You need to resolve to adjust your ways
When the motive is then unveiled.

These close encounters with what's inside
Will give you a chance to grow.
They offer the opportunity then,
Your inner self to know.

The experience, though unpleasant and sad,
Will keep you dependent on God.
It will give you a taste of humility,
When facing your false facade.

For men seem to have a tendency,
When under life's pressure to act,
To choose a way that's convenient for self,
Rather than facing the facts.

It came on the heels of Adam's choice,
But that's why the Savior has died,
To give us the victory to conquer ourselves,
The conscience to rectify.

Then go to Him now; He's opened the way
For you to find comfort and peace.
Lay it all on the table; He's promised to help,
If you will your problem release.

And if you are tempted to do it again,
Whatever the problem may be,
He'll show you the way to escape it today
And will give you the victory.

Contentment

Since each person is unique, there's no reason now to seek
To be envious of someone you admire,
For it's better to be happy with the gifts you have been lent,
Than to live with bleak, unsatisfied desire.

If you tend to envy those who have fancy toys or clothes,
Just remember that their outward show may hide,
All the problems they may know which they seldom care to show,
While they keep their disappointment all inside.

It's a hard but useful lesson that each one is slow to learn,
To accept the things with which you have been blessed,
To develop talents given, not by envy to be driven,
Choosing not to be discouraged or distressed.

If there's one whom you would copy, let it be the Lord above,
Whose desire it was to make of all a friend,
Who rejoiced to help another, whether sister or a brother,
Blessing all who needed hope to start again.

For when focus is on self, on acquirements, or on wealth,
Discontent will rob you of intended joy,
Be determined to be happy with the talents which are yours,
And you'll rise above the things which may annoy.

Courage

Courage is the will to do the thing which you may fear,
To gather all the strength you have when challenges are near.
Courage isn't for the soul who never took a stand,
Nor is it for the one who seeks escape from heaven's plan.

It took some courage long ago when Noah built the ark,
For he had never seen it rain, yet on God's word embarked.
It also took some fortitude for Abraham to leave
The country that he knew so well, another to receive.

The Israelites of Moses' time found courage at the sea,
To step into the water, the Egyptians troops to flee.
Queen Esther had the courage, when her life was on the line,
To speak up for God's people, their future to define.

And then there were the Hebrew men who wouldn't bend the knees,
To worship a statue made of gold, a haughty king to please.
When Daniel refused to cease to pray when threatened with his death,
He was thrown into a den of lions, subjected to feel their breath.

It takes a bit of courage when you're called upon to stand,
For things that are important, which derive from heaven's plan.
But as you follow the Spirit's lead, God's will to thus explore,
You'll find by walking in His will, new strength not known before.

Covering of White

The falling snow lends qualities that put the soul at peace.
Its constancy while falling can offer sweet release.
The pristine white uplifts the heart while covering the earth,
Enveloping the barren hills and giving them new birth.

No manmade scars or blemishes appear to mar the show,
As all things disappear beneath the blanket white of snow.
And as I gaze in wonder from my window safe inside,
Its veil of white and purity suggests a virgin bride.

For we are all the bride of Christ who dare to take His name,
He gives us garments pure and white to wash away our shame.
He bids us wear His robe of white and leave our past behind,
That we in Him may represent new life that one may find.

Crossroads

Where are you headed while going through life?
What are you focused on, friend?
Are you seeking the things that pertain to this life,
On the things that will come to an end?

Though some things are needed, yet most things are not,
We waste too much time on the latter,
We would be better off in choosing those things
Which in time will essentially matter.

We run here and there, in pursuit and in care,
Seeking that which will last for a while,
While time rushes on and soon will be gone,
As we strive in the rank and the file.

Each man is apportioned a time in the sun
To discover the role he should play,
Results will be seen in the choices he's made,
When he comes to the end of the day.

It won't be acquirements of houses or lands,
Fine clothing, or highest position,
That spell his success or how he is blessed
When weighed in his final condition.

As someone once noted, we lay waste our powers
In getting and spending while here,
For Instead of attending to things of true worth,
We accept the thing that is near.

A word to encourage, a stand for the right,
A smile for the lonely and sad,
A helping hand offered to those found in need,
Will make the heart healthy and glad.

Devotion to family in time and in prayer,
The bending of knee to our God,
The willing obedience to all His commands
Will point out what's good on earth's sod.

Don't wait till the hairs on your head turn to grey
To discern what's important to know,
But cherish the meaningful values today
By choosing the best way to go.

For God in His wisdom, out of love for your choice,
Has given two options to man,
He never coerces the soul or the mind,
But prays you will follow His plan.

For nothing else matters when all's said and done,
The future is set by the past,
And only the things that are valued by God
Are those that are destined to last.

Choose wisely today as you go on your way,
Make God your companion and friend,
By abiding in Him, other things will grow dim,
You'll be sure to succeed in the end.

Dark Gethsemane

We celebrate the special day that marked the Savior's rising,
The fact that we have chosen to is really not surprising.
It truly was remarkable and totally unsurpassed,
It marked the day that gave man hope that eternity would last.

Though this event is highly praised and rightfully should be,
The victory for salvation's hope occurred in Gethsemane.
For it was there that Jesus prayed and sweat great drops of blood,
He struggled with man's heavy guilt to overcome sin's flood.

He longed for His disciples through that time of darkest night,
To pray with Him for needed strength, while he prayed, out of sight.
They knew that He seemed burdened, but they quickly fell asleep,
While the future of the race was forged within the garden deep.

If only they had spent the time in earnest, fervent prayer,
They would have been more fortified, the Master's grief to bear.
Instead, they fled when trouble came and left Him all alone,
While He would end up on the cross and for their sins atone.

How is it now with you, my friend? Do you share God's love for man?
And have you thus aligned yourself, according to God's plan?
For it was there among the trees of dark Gethsemane,
That the Son of God surrendered all to die for you and me.

Deception

Deception is a funny thing; it's hard to recognize.
It catches people unaware and takes them by surprise.
It started in a garden small so many years ago,
Where Eve was tempted by a snake whose colors did not show.

It sneaks around, pretending that it has your good in mind,
While all the time its tentacles around you seem to wind.
It offers all the pleasant things that seem to fit your fancy,
But choosing what it offers you is always somewhat chancy.

You'll find that it is subtle; your reaction is to prize it,
Until you study heaven's book with which to recognize it.
You'll find that you are up against a mean and mighty foe,
Who prizes your destruction and will yield a final blow.

He often takes the Word of God and seasons it with lies,
By twisting it to say some things that never were implied.
The only safe avoidance from this weapon that he uses,
Is favoring the Word of God in everything one chooses.

It isn't safe to trust one's mind; deception is alive,
It takes reliance on God's Word for one to now survive.
Then pray for God to lead you by His Spirit as you read.
By feasting on His written Word, you surely will succeed.

Decisions

What are you doing for Jesus today?
Are you styling your life after Him?
Or are you engaging in worldly pursuits
And causing your light to grow dim?

You consented at one time to give Him your all,
But distractions have come in between,
Is your future goal heaven, or are you concerned
With only the things that are seen?

There's a heaven to win and a hell to be shunned,
God's coming is not far away,
Are you making decisions and planning your life
To be used for His glory today?

For if you're not sure what He'd have you to do,
Why not make it an object of prayer?
He'll lead you by circumstance, conscience, and love,
For He said He will always be there.

As men turn from God and pursue their own ways,
God's Spirit withdraws from the earth,
While Satan steps in to enslave men in sin
And to rob them of things of true worth.

He causes destruction, confusion, and death
By earthquakes, and flooding, and fire,
He stirs up the people in protests on streets,
Each seeking a selfish desire.

It soon will be over; make sure you confirm
That it's on the Lord's side you will stand,
For it's either from Satan or God, by your choice,
You have chosen to take a command.

There's no middle ground; your decision today
Will propose what your future will be,
This old earth is fading and soon will be gone,
So decide for eternity.

Default System

Default is automatic mode when systems are in place,
It regulates the course of things and will all else replace.
The system we inherited derived from Adam's choice,
When in the garden long ago, he heeded Satan's voice.

God made of Adam and his wife a rather small request,
One tree, which they were not to eat, was placed there as a test.
Though other fruit was theirs to eat, when God provided choice,
Instead of their obedience, they heeded Satan's voice.

Their perfect robes of sinless light evaporated there,
They felt the atmosphere turn cool and noticed they were bare.
Their modus operandi of perfect love and joy,
Defaulted to another mode which would their souls destroy.

They found, when challenges arose, or when they made decisions,
Their hearts were turned to selfishness, despising supervision.
But God can change the selfish heart and soften it with love,
Returning man to God's default, which comes from up above.

So where is your default today—with Adam or with Christ?
To give up self and humble be can seem a hefty price.
Though you may stumble on the way, if Christ is your default,
He'll take on Satan in your heart and conquer his assaults.

Drawing Warmth

What will you do when rejection arrives
And the world turns against you in hate?
When the things you believe are hard to conceive
By the world and are up for debate?

The challenge will come if you're true to God's Word,
If you stand for the right in this world,
For then when you do, you will find that it's true,
That Satan's wrath will unfurl.

This comes as a challenge, no matter how firm
You've decided in heart you will be,
And you only will stand by the strength of God's hand,
And it's then that His might you will see.

Drawing warmth from the coldness of others that day
Will not be a comfortable task,
But with God on your side, in His arms you'll abide,
And His love is the thing that will last.

You must look past the challenge that then will arise,
To the future that God has prepared.
What you hold in your hand, men will not understand,
Though with each man God's word has been shared.

Every soul will either accept or reject
Heaven's treasure that's brought to his door.
He can throw it away or value each day
Every gem that God's Word has in store.

With His courage, stay strong and resist what is wrong,
Standing true to God's Word that you know.
In the end you'll receive heaven's robe of pure white,
For your witness on earth below.

Emmanuel, God with Us

A thing that will engage the mind and fascinate the thought,
Is how the King of heaven for the men on earth has wrought.
For when the creatures God had made chose poorly and were lost,
He sacrificed the One He treasured most at utmost cost.

Eternity held them closely, while working hand in hand,
Upholding all the worlds above and making noble plans.
Though each, an individual, yet thinking as the One,
Their hearts were knit together: the Father and the Son.

Yet when the plan unfurled for man, by God's premeditation,
The Two who knew eternity would suffer separation.
Emmanuel, God with us, became that costly gift,
As Christ endured the wretched cross, providing men a lift.

He wasn't just man's Savior then, but He was God with us,
Forever linked to mankind as the Godhead had discussed.
When dying there upon the cross, Christ felt the darkness grow,
As separation from the Father crushed His heart below.

Unending joy should thrill each soul at what the Two have done,
In giving us this gift of love: the Father's only Son.
Emmanuel, God with us, our song will ever be,
As we enjoy this precious Gift for all eternity.

Emotional Intelligence

What is your emotional intelligence today,
On a scale of one to ten?
Are you willing to give up a present delight
For rewards that the future will send?

Or are you a lot like some children you know,
When given the option and baited,
Who will gobble a small bit of candy at once,
When told there was more if they'd waited?

Like children, we often are ready to grasp
The things that at first may appeal,
While giving no heed to the options that rise,
Which a quick choice may then from us steal.

We go into debt for the notions we crave,
Which we think we just have to have now,
Which are often discarded and trashed in time
When before our desires we have bowed.

This immediate gratification of men
Carries over to spiritual things,
In which we will choose our present desires
Over that which the future will bring.

We're reluctant to use self denial today,
To forego present joys for tomorrow,
Instead, we may choose before thinking it out,
Which only brings trouble and sorrow.

If lacking faith, we're not willing to wait
For the heavenly, promised reward,
And to forego immediate pleasure today,
Which in time, we will have to discard.

It's better to wait for tomorrow, my friend,
In which best dreams of God are fulfilled,
Instead of relying on pleasures of earth,
Which in time, this old world will have killed.

Enigma in Flesh

When Christ descended from heaven to earth,
He was found as a mystery.
He was totally human, yet totally God,
He was quite an enigma, you see.

Though His heavenly glory was shrouded from men,
To keep them from being distracted,
Yet divinity flashed through His action at times,
Which only the mystery compacted.

He depended on God, His Father, above,
Giving men an example while here,
Though He lived not for self, laying power on the shelf,
Yet for others, His power drew near.

He threw Himself willingly into the soil,
Of the world's great, desperate need,
He became the great seed that would flourish and feed,
Willing souls by His words and His deeds.

With this mystery divine that boggles the mind,
We only can wonder, amazed,
For in being the pattern by which we must live,
He, to heaven, a highway has blazed.

Though He took on humanity when at its worse,
Yet He stooped not to wallow in sin,
Not a blot could be found in His being profound,
But only a heart pure within.

What a Savior is mine, this being divine,
Who was willing to hang on a cross,
For in anguish and shame, He took all my blame,
In love for my soul, which was lost.

Can you turn Him away, this Savior today,
This One who was willing to die?
Praise God up in heaven, His grace is sufficient,
For you and for folks such as I.

Enigmas

An enigma is a curious thing and even seems ironic,
It always is unusual and never often chronic.
An egret is a fine example of this wondrous thing,
For from his nose down to his toes, he's clean out to the wing.

It doesn't matter whether he's in rain or sunshine bright,
Though he may stand in muddy fields, he's always pristine white.
A pig could take a lesson here about some cleanliness,
And while he's at it, learn a thing about some true finesse.

The egret is a bird to note, wherever he may be,
But how he tends to stay so clean appears a mystery.
A swan is also much the same and is a graceful sight,
The fact that both appear so clean becomes a fair delight.

I guess I'll never know for sure just how they seem to manage,
But for the folks who study them, it seems a great advantage.
Another great enigma is how God can take a soul,
Whose heart is dark with grime and sin and make him clean and whole.

Though enigmas are a mystery, I'm glad that they exist,
Especially when God's Spirit speaks and man does not resist.
For that is the greatest mystery, and though I don't understand,
I'm thankful for this miracle: the touch of the Master's hand.

Enoch

Enoch was a son of God who lived in early times,
He walked upon this earthly sod through varied scenes and climes.
He knew of Adam's tragic fall and viewed the sad effects,
He saw the wickedness which grew from evil men's defects.

He sorrowed for the sins of men and sought a better way,
He tried his best to please the Lord throughout his humble day.
He sought to turn men's hearts to God and often would correct
Their evil ways in hopes that they would on their lives reflect.

He lived so closely to the Lord in prayer and meditation,
That God revealed to him the plans He'd made for His creation.
He showed him visions of the world unto the end of time,
And how the world would then be filled with wickedness and crime.

God showed him how He planned to come in glorious array,
And how innumerable angel hosts would come with Him that day.
And after Enoch had a son, his understanding grew,
He sympathized with God above when a father's heart he knew.

He faithfully continued on, revealing God to men,
Reminding them of heaven's love and the Savior God would send.
He lived so close to God in life that on a chosen day,
God whisked him up to live above, far from the earth away.

And like this son of long ago, we too must share God's love
With folks around and be prepared to go to heaven above.
For nothing less will satisfy the goals God has in mind,
And if you seek Him faithfully, God's paradise you'll find.

Escape to the Light

What do you do when the weight of the world,
In darkness has gathered around,
When tragedies both that are near and afar,
Have entered your life to surround?

What can you do when the tables are turned,
When people despise what is right,
When the way to solve problems is to blame someone else,
Or take to the sidewalks and fight?

When the news of the day features horror and blood,
From the senseless shootings that grow,
When personal tragedy strikes at your door,
There's something I think you should know.

This war between good and evil commenced,
In a world that existed above,
It was joyful and perfect till sin entered in,
And challenged the Father of love.

God labored at length with this angel of light,
Who wouldn't repent of rebellion,
At last, he was thrown out of heaven above,
Becoming the first tragic hellion.

The war continues on earth to this day,
The news will attest to this fact,
For evil continues to grow in men's hearts,
Exposing their spiritual lack.

So don't be surprised when the darkness surrounds,
When you don't know which way you should turn.
The only solution available now,
Is to open your Bible and learn.

For God has provided a way of escape,
From the darkness and into His light,
He has conquered the dark by His death on the cross,
And by living a life that was right.

His gift of a perfect life can be yours,
If you will accept of His gift,
He will guide you through darkness and into His light,
The balance of power to shift.

Then go to Him now, before Him to bow,
Confess all your sins and repent,
You'll rejoice in the freedom and joy He bestows,
In the wonderful gift He has sent.

Everlasting Covenant

When God established His covenant with Abraham of old,
He emphasized His sovereignty in letters strong and bold.
The everlasting covenant that to mankind then was made,
Became the great assurance of the price that would be paid.

A seed to him was promised by whom all men would be blessed,
In gaining man's salvation to secure eternal rest.
The problem was that Abraham and Sarah both were old,
And far beyond conception years, if truth must now be told.

They staggered at God's promises and only half believed,
That at their age and time of life that Sarah could conceive.
They thought to help the thing along and offered Sarah's maid,
To be a mother to the child and thus, God's plan to aid.

That soon became a problem when some jealousy appeared,
As Hagar mocked the motherless, which summoned Sarah's tears.
Both Hagar then and Ishmael were banished far away,
In God's own time, the promised child was born, as God did say.

Then circumcision came about as God's rebuke to man,
To teach him that all things must be according to God's plan.
Abram was retested then so that the Lord might see,
If he would yield his will to God and thus, would faithful be.

God asked his servant Abraham to take this promised seed,
And offer him as sacrifice—a daunting, frightening deed.
Would Abraham now pass this test, and would he faithful be,
To carry out the Lord's command, despite his hesitancy?

Though Abram's heart was heavy at the prospect he must face,
The Bible states that he complied and conquered through God's grace.
For as he held the knife above to bravely thrust it in,
The Lord would intercept the act to save men from their sin.

A ram who roamed the hills that day became the sacrifice,
Which typified the Savior's death to save from sin and vice.
And Abram's son would represent the plight of humankind,
Whose destiny was surely death, which each in time would find.

And Abraham became a type of the Father up above,
Who offered Jesus willingly because of heaven's love.
Behold God's Gift, displayed in type that we might understand,
The heavy price that love would pay for every sinful man.

The covenant then was ratified but not by man's device,
But by the Father's loving gift of Jesus' sacrifice.
Though man would fail to play his part, yet God would salvage all,
Redeeming man from certain death, resulting from his fall.

Fallen From Grace

What can you do when falling from grace
While walking in willful ways?
What are the only two choices you have
That will count in the future days?

You can wander around in discouragement bound,
With conscience condemning you now,
Or you can determine new choices to make,
When low before Jesus you bow.

For all of us stumble from selfish desires,
Enticed by a sinful temptation,
But how we react when we stumble and fall
Will determine our destination.

We can choose to continue our self-serving acts,
Contented to wallow in sin,
Or we can confess our transgressions to God
Who can give us contentment within.

We can justify all of our sinful mistakes
Or face up to what we have done,
Admitting the course we have taken is wrong,
Regretting the course we have run.

We need to acknowledge that we're in a war,
And only one side will succeed,
The course that we take has eternal results
As determined by words and by deeds.

God loves you, desiring the best you can be,
You must dedicate all that you are.
He can tell where your choices are leading today,
He can study your future afar.

Don't ever suppose you're too evil to change,
For God can work miracles yet,
Your only disaster in fighting the war
Is in choosing the Lord to forget.

Fear Not

Don't bother to be anxious or be filled with anxious gloom,
For Jesus knew you long before He knit you in the womb.
Though darkness seems to close you in, don't give in to despair,
Whatever you are going through, God's promised to be there.

He had your purpose well in mind before the world began,
He's given you a place in life like each and every man.
He wants for you to walk with Him in this old world below,
He knows the very place you live and people you may know.

Though joy may be obstructed by the obstacles you meet,
Remember there is healing at the Savior's precious feet,
He's reaching out to take your hand, that He may show the way,
Surrender all your fears to Him and walk with Him today.

Fear, a Conquered Foe

Fear is a tool of the devil to eclipse the Word of God,
As we travel on our journey here upon this earthly sod.
It causes hope to vanish and our joy to disappear,
Allowing faith to fade away and be replaced with fear.

Don't let this strong temptation now extinguish heaven's light,
Or cause your feet to wander far from championing the right.
But lift your thoughts to heaven above and dwell on what is fair,
Remembering whatever comes that God is always there.

Let not the night of terror wreak its havoc in the soul,
But summon God's artillery at once to take control.
Remember, God is greater far than all the devil's powers,
And He will keep your soul from fear throughout the lonely hours.

Then call on God, whose victory over fear was at the cross,
Whose love for you and me was greater than His personal loss,
That in His conquest, we may rise to claim the victory, too,
Expelling every fear that may arise in me and you.

Food for Thought

Why settle for the crumbs you find when you could have a meal?
Some things one finds to snack upon lack nourishing appeal.
A movie here, a novel there, a fantasy unreal,
Will have no lasting value though your fancy it may steal.

Some healthy food that feeds the mind is found in God's own Word.
Too much of what we now consume is foolish or absurd.
For we become what we ingest, though it be books or food,
And by beholding, we are changed by that on which we brood.

Two forces in the world exist that differ from each other,
Your choice will be for one of them—you will not find another.
Don't waste your time with foolish things, for life is brief at best,
But choose the things that feed the soul before you take your rest.

Force

If force becomes a weapon that is needed for a cause,
Then the cause is found deplete of vital power.
For the winning force of love, which derives from God above,
Is a virtue that will conquer and will flower.

For love provides a freedom that will give the soul a choice;
Forced obedience declares a cause is weak.
Using force just proves the point that the cause will not survive,
For its only goal is power, which it seeks.

The force that grows and lasts and will finally be sustained
Is the one that will exist by words of truth.
The only motives guiding those resorting then to force,
Will be found to be unfair and less than couth.

God's willingness to die and display His selflessness,
Is a force that woos and wins the needy heart.
Though force may bring compliance, a rebellion settles in,
Which will drive a cause and victim far apart.

For selfishness and pride occupy the very root,
From which force and its contingencies are grown.
In the end, it's doomed to die, by refusing to rely,
On the virtues which belong to God alone.

You will find that brute coercion is the weapon that is found,
In the arsenal of weak and fearful men.
Since they know their cause is weak, other methods they will seek,
Hoping by their use, their causes to defend.

Beware of any cause that sanctions use of brutal force,
In which rightful choice of men has been denied.
If the precious right to choose is allowed to be abused,
You will know that heaven's patience has been tried.

The use of undue force designates a downward course,
When it subjugates the consciences of men,
For when Jesus comes again and with judgment comes to reign,
It's the right to choose that heaven will defend.

Freedom's Song

I sing a song of freedom, of forgiveness from the past,
A reconciliation with my Savior, which I know will last.
Broken are the shackles that had bound me as a slave,
Banished by the hope of heaven which the Savior gave.

Resentment and old bitterness had torn my spirit down,
Until I gazed on Calvary and saw Christ's thorny crown.
Relinquishing the unforgiving anger in my soul,
I now surrender to the One who makes the sinner whole.

I sing a song of freedom now; no grudges weigh me down.
I've found that life is much too short by anger to be bound.
I open up my heart to those who may have done me wrong,
And by God's mercy and His grace, I sing new freedom's song.

Each man I meet is valued now as one more child of God,
Awaiting invitation to the joy of Eden's sod.
Then let me share this freedom with the souls that I may meet,
That they may also bask in freedom found at Jesus' feet.

Fundraising God's Way

While building a place of worship, when Moses needed donations,
He didn't plan a party for outward motivation.
He provided no games to entice, nor bribed with food to eat,
He didn't seek entertainment or convince with something sweet.

He merely presented the need, so men could decide in their heart,
What gift that they would contribute to play a helpful part.
Though other methods might work, in bringing donations in,
God wanted their freewill offerings, no selfish gain to win.

For the proper motivation, is not to get but to give,
Other methods are unacceptable and are not God's way to live.
The only proper donation is one that comes from the heart,
Reconsider your plans and actions; from selfishness depart.

The principle in our giving, whether for church or school,
Should be a freewill offering, which always is the rule.
Then search your heart today; allow no compromise,
For giving so you can get is never right or wise.

For God can't bless the funds which are raised by selfish gain,
By involving ourselves in this, we ignore what God makes plain.
If there is a need, just ask, and funds will come pouring in,
From the grateful hearts of those who now desire God's favor to win.

Garments of Light

Nakedness is a result of sin,
For back in the garden fair,
Adam and Eve wore garments of light,
While dwelling in innocence there.

It was only when sin had entered in,
That they lost their garments of light,
They discovered that they were naked then,
Bereft of coverings bright.

They hid themselves and in its place,
They sewed a garment of leaves,
They tried to cover their loss of light
After the pair were deceived.

When God came along at the evening hour,
He called to His creatures there,
And when He observed the flimsy clothes,
He provided them garments of hair.

He covered them with an animal skin,
And blood was shed with its loss,
Which symbolized the sacrifice
That Christ would make on the cross.

It's a trait of fallen humankind
To try to cover their sins,
With vain attempts at flimsy leaves
Instead of changes within.

For man will try to make things right
By pain and flagellation,
As if the work that he can do
Will offer him salvation.

The answer to this problem sore
That badgers every man,
Is found in his acceptance of Christ,
And His one and only plan.

For the robe of perfect righteousness
Has no thread of man's own making,
And it's only through Jesus' sacrifice
That His robe is there for the taking.

For when a man enters the city above,
The only robe that will do,
Is the robe of Christ's own righteousness,
Offered to me and to you.

Gift of the Snake

Though death and taxes seem to be the lot of every man,
You need to know that death itself was not in heaven's plan.
When man decided to turn from God and listen to the snake,
He suddenly changed his destiny, not dreaming hell was at stake.

The choice to disobey God's word is always a risky thing,
For man has little knowledge of the pain his choice will bring.
When choosing to learn of evil that day as if it were a prize,
Man turned saway from what was good and thus, God's word despised.

The choice would bring a world of hurt of sickness, pain, and death,
Which was guaranteed to every man before he took a breath.
Because man thought he was missing out on something good overlooked,
He turned from God to deal with a snake and thus, God's word forsook.

It seemed a little thing that day, for all was sweetness and light,
Yet nothing like the choice man made would offer such a blight.
For any deviation from the counsel God has sent,
Will bring about a consequence that is on evil bent.

Be careful of your choice today, and think before you leap,
Or you may be discouraged with results that you may reap.
The last foe that will be destroyed will be the one of death,
When God once more will reinstate the joy of heaven's breath.

God's Ambassador

No greater prophet has ever lived,
Than John, the cousin of Christ,
And because of his truth and faithfulness,
His life was a sacrifice.

He lived a sober existence alone
And dwelt in the bleak wilderness,
His mission of being God's messenger
Was the cherished one he possessed.

From childhood on, he looked for Christ
To fulfill what he had been shown,
For he had been given a sign by which
The Messiah would then be known.

When the time was right, with the Jordan near,
He gave the call to repent,
To rich and poor, both young and old,
His message then was sent.

When Christ came by, He asked of John
To baptize Him as well,
And when he did, John saw the sign,
As a dove upon Christ fell.

He recognized the Son of God
And protested to serve Him there,
For he felt unworthy, Christ's shoes to unlatch,
Much less this honor to share.

When Christ insisted, he baptized Him,
And when from the water, Christ rose,
John cried, "Behold the Lamb of God!"
For it was a scene grandiose.

As the Savior's ministry started to grow,
He knew that John's would wane,
John's disciples, while noting this obvious fact,
Began to moan and complain.

"He must increase, but I must decrease",
John answered to settle the case.
From that day on, Christ's ministry grew,
While John's would be replaced.

When King Herod took his brother's wife,
John chastened him for this act,
And as a result, from envy and hate,
John's death became a fact.

But while in prison, awaiting his death,
John sent his disciples to ask,
If Jesus was really Messiah to come,
While John was taken to task.

Christ did not directly give answer to them,
But told John's disciples to tell,
Of the wonderful things they had witnessed that day,
In making the people well.

John died at the hands of a desperate king
When he died as a martyr that day,
But he saw his commission would be fulfilled,
For Messiah was on His way.

We don't know for certain if John was among
The people who rose with the Christ,
But we know he will rise when Jesus returns,
And that is enough to suffice.

God's Commandments

As you may note, the Ten Commandments aren't just suggestions,
The fact that they were placed in stone should silence any questions.
The Bible says by breaking one, you've broken all the rest,
Yet mankind has neglected one: the day that God has blessed.

The Sabbath day was made for man to worship his Creator,
By putting Sunday in its place, the church became a traitor.
No man has the authority to change God's law and day,
For God has said He changes not, despite what man may say.

For Sunday was the pagan day the heathen kept of old,
The church proposed this compromise to get them in the fold.
Then many other compromises followed in its train,
The church became like Babylon, and evil came to reign.

Because of persecution's ire, the truth went underground,
Yet faithful souls in secrecy would keep it still around.
But with the coming of the light, God's truth is now reclaimed,
By those who keep the Sabbath truth in honor of God's name.

There is no validation in God's Word to change the day,
The Roman Emperor Constantine did thus lead men astray.
It then became a manmade day in place of God's command,
In spite of this, the Word of God forevermore will stand.

Though Sunday now is widely held by those who once protested
The days of dark atrocities that history has attested.
The Bible says God's Sabbath day will be a test in time,
The choice will be to follow men or worship God sublime.

God chooses not to force His will; the choice is yours today,
To follow Him because of love or go your separate way.
But in the end, you'll find it's true, when heaven has begun,
We'll keep His day as He commands: the holy, seventh one.

God's Day

When God first blessed the seventh day, He didn't mean the sixth,
He didn't mean the day of the sun or any day betwixt,
For God is most particular and says He will not change,
There is no room for man's ideas to try to rearrange.

Yet willful man will have his way when under sin's control,
His own ideas will try to trump the Lord's with notions bold,
Yet God will not be trifled with, and He will have His way,
And man will bend to heaven's will when comes the judgment day.

Though folks may choose to worship God upon another day,
There 's only one that God has blessed, despite what man may say.
If God had changed His sacred day, the Bible would commend it,
Although you search on every page, no text will now defend it.

Consider well what you will choose, for only one is right,
It pays to be on heaven's side and not the Lord to fight,
For there's a heaven to be won, and there's a hell to shun,
And all will worship on God's day once heaven has begun.

God's Judgments

Though men may question God's resolves as they on earth abide,
His ways are unimpeachable; he has no need to hide.
Decisions, when examined, will reveal a full disclosure,
When subject to the scrutiny of absolute exposure.

When Jesus takes the righteous ones to sit with Him on thrones,
A thousand years are given them to search the books He owns.
The records are de-classified; no hidden things are there,
And as they read His record books, the judgments found are fair.

God deals in truth and honesty; He deals not in deception,
Since He has nothing there to hide, it cancels misperception.
God passes judgment to the Son, who then will pass it on,
For man's review and scrutiny, for all to dwell upon.

He gives men time for all to see how righteous He has ruled,
And how, because of Satan's lies, men often have been fooled.
Until the universe as one, the wicked and the good,
Confess with one resounding voice, God judged men as He should.

God's Love

God's love is like a shining light that points the way to home,
A GPS that never fails, no matter where you roam.
God's love is like a gentle breeze that soothes all doubts and fears,
A calming peace that quiets anxious moments, marked by tears.

His love is like a healing balm when wounds need time and care,
It satisfies the hurt and sting that often lingers there.
His love is like a drink in time when water is the need,
When nothing else can satisfy or thus the longing feed.

His love is like the bread of life that fills the hungry soul,
That satisfies the deepest need and makes the body whole.
His love is like a cooling bath that washes care away,
Refreshing and reviving one to face another day.

God's love is like the anchor set within the storm that blows,
That keeps the soul from crashing on the rocks where dangers pose.
His love encircles every man, awaiting a return,
From those for whom His heart of love will always, ever yearn.

God's Majestic Power

"By the word of the Lord were the heavens made",
He didn't need material,
For when He spoke, creation appeared,
Including things ethereal.

His limitless power is observed in the sky,
Where He guides each star through space.
His power and majesty stir each heart,
That would know His loving embrace.

He cared for His people in ages past,
And provided their needs for each day.
He led them to safety from Pharaoh's assault,
By drying the sea on their way.

Through thunder and lightning, He issued commands,
Writing them down with His finger.
From a burning bush, He gave Moses a push,
When he was inclined to linger.

At the tower of Babel, when men became proud,
God did all their language confuse.
He spoke through a donkey, His prophet to guide,
When the prophet, God's creature abused.

When Jericho fell, that city of old,
It wasn't by man's intuition.
But the walls tumbled down, and the battle was won,
Because of God's guiding commission.

When three Hebrew worthies refused to bow down,
To a statue to honor a king,
They were thrown in a fire because of man's ire,
Yet God would deliverance bring.

God showed men the future by Joseph's two dreams,
Which seemed an unusual deed,
Yet things came together, God's people to save,
When there was a critical need.

God said He is building a city above,
Where sorrow will never arise.
His power will shine in the new world we find,
As we wing our way up through the skies.

For there's nothing in heaven or earth, God can't do,
His power, He loves to impart.
And the greatest display of His power and love,
Is in changing the human heart.

God's Man

I wish to be like Paul, God's man, with bold, courageous tone,
Who did not fear the daunting act of standing all alone.
Misguided first, and apt to kill, yet bold to save at last,
He focused on the rising goal, decrying what was past.

Bereft by light of earthly sight while on a ghastly mission,
He pondered well his sordid past, receiving new commission.
Now humbled in his helpless state, and redirected thus,
He morphed into a noble man, into new mission thrust.

No longer would he persecute believers in The Way,
But would their Lord exonerate through obstacles' array.
Once seeing Christ and hearing of His words from heaven's court,
His mind became their citadel, their essence now his fort.

He felt their weight upon his mind; God's words became His guide,
And naught from king nor prisoner would he, their message hide.
Though beaten by his enemies and left by them for dead,
God raised him up to speak for Him, no countenance to dread.

Surrounded by his enemies, who sought to do him in,
He stood for truth and righteousness and warned them of their sin.
New struggles rose at every turn, yet he with courage stood,
By witnessing of Jesus Christ, he gathered whom he could.

He died at last a martyr's death, his mission all completed,
Rejoicing in the victory from the foe whom God defeated.
May we in faith who read Paul's words unto this very day,
With gratitude, new courage find to follow in God's way.

God's Plans

When Stephen went before the proud Sanhedrin to be tried,
He spoke of Jewish history and how Jesus was denied.
In anger, they accused him and condemned him in their pride,
They wrestled with their consciences, which they could not abide.

They stoned him with hostility, but what they never knew,
Was that their persecution would incite an era new.
For as the Christians fled from home and scattered here and there,
The news of Jesus' gospel would be taken everywhere.

For when the devil thought to kill the gospel by this deed,
God used it to advantage then to plant the gospel seed.
And so today, the things that seem to lead one to despair,
The Lord can use to turn around and help a person there.

He has a plan for every life, and he can take the bad,
And though sometimes we may not see, He'll turn it into glad.
Don't ever take your eyes from Him; in time He'll make it plain,
That all things work together, and your joy will yet remain.

God's Precious Promises

How precious are the promises that hide within God's Word,
When sought and found, they will the hope of seekers undergird.
The promises are guaranteed because God never lies.
They cover every human life and every need supply.

If you are lonely, God has promised He is always there,
He's promised that He'll never leave; He knows your every care.
If you will be obedient, God promises His peace,
And treasures up in heaven where the time will never cease.

If you own little in this world, it will not always be,
For God has riches stored for you, which no one else can see.
If you are meek and think your life to be of little worth,
God promises you will in time inherit all the earth.

When you decide to cherish God, He'll grant your heart's desires,
He's promised to deliver you from Satan's wrath and ire.
If you will have humility, then God will lift you up,
He'll honor you and make you rich by filling up your cup.

It takes a little faith to wait, God's promises to see,
For some may not come right away but may come gradually.
If God sees best to hold them now, it may be just a test,
But if you will but trust His Word, you'll find that He knows best.

God's Promises

The promises of God are true and righteous altogether,
They stand intact for those who claim, despite the mood or weather.
Since they are based upon God's Word, fulfillment is assured,
They stand as firm as steel or rock, and thus, their truth endures.

God's promises are likened to the rudder on a boat,
Which is designed to steer the ship when once it is afloat.
The promises are also like the water to the seed,
Which offers proper nourishment in answer to its need.

God's promises can be compared to signposts on the way,
Which bring the weary traveler home at closing of the day.
They also are exemplified by wind beneath the wing,
That wills the soul to fly above the world's depressing things.

The promises of God are like a strong and mighty tree,
That sends its roots into the ground, to seal its destiny.
The promises are like a lamp that sheds its searching light,
And spreads its welcome beams abroad within the darkest night.

The promises of God endure like crocus in the snow,
Which bloom in spite of winter's cold, God's loving care to show.
The promises can be compared to flowers in the spring,
Which grow and nod in warming sun, new peace and hope to bring.

God's promises are free to claim when men His laws obey,
They're offered to the willing souls who choose to walk His way.
Then be assured while claiming them, for God will back His Word,
For they declare a guarantee, which heaven undergirds.

God's Robe of Love

The fine, woven garment of righteousness
Is a product of God's own making.
It's bestowed on man as a special gift
Of God's own undertaking.

When mankind lost their robe of light
By sin in the garden fair,
They tried to cover their nakedness
With fig leaves that were there.

But only the loom of heaven above
Could replace such a garment or gift,
For the bent of man is to stumble and fall
To wander from God and drift.

So a Savior was sent to recover the light,
Which man's transgression had lost,
His perfect life would restore the gift
By His death on the infamous cross.

The robe is not given to cover the sins
Which are cherished by evil men,
But man can be covered by clinging to Christ
And starting with new life again.

For it's not in oneself that its strength can be found,
But in looking to Jesus above,
Who offered His own perfect life in our place,
And gives us His robe with His love.

God's Sacred Word

God's love was written out for us as plainly as could be,
He placed the final period when He died on Calvary.
The Scriptures are His written Word that never has grown old,
Which Jesus always magnified on earth in actions bold.

The rules that show God's will for us are written in His law,
Which then reflect His character, which angels hold in awe.
God's rules are not suggestions to accept or just ignore,
Their keeping seals our happiness and future fate in store.

When God has told us what to do, He's knows what's for our best,
No substitute that man has made can then be good or blessed.
When tempted in the wilderness, Christ's victory was secured,
By quoting well-known Scriptures as temptation He endured.

Our only safety in this world from Satan and deceptions,
Is just to know what Jesus said, allowing no exceptions.
We will not know God's will for us unless we take the time,
To study what the Scriptures teach and read His Word sublime.

It doesn't matter what you've heard upon this earthly sod,
The only thing that matters is the sacred Word of God.
For deception will be peddled, and the only way to know,
Is to follow God completely that your faith in Him may grow.

God's Seventh Day

Why do I worship on Saturday; why do I kneel and pray?
God says the seventh day is His, which I should then obey.
God put a special blessing on this day at the beginning,
Before a Jew was ever born or man conceived of sinning.

He blessed the day when earth was made in honor of His name,
So men would not forget the day or Him from whom they came.
He later said to "Remember" it, and wrote it down in stone,
So men would not forget the fact that He was God alone.

According to the words He spoke, God says He doesn't change,
Although mankind has tried its best, God's words to rearrange.
You cannot change what God has blessed, no matter what men say,
And even the resurrection is no cause to change the day.

For Jesus worshipped on this day when He was here on earth,
He never mentioned another one as being of special worth.
His own disciples never thought to follow another day,
And even after Jesus died, they followed in His way.

The day is not in question, as the Jews still keep this day,
Although its Lord and Master, they rejected and put away.
Authority is the question here—will it be God's or man's?
Your answer to this question now will indicate your stand.

Jesus said He was Lord of the Sabbath, and He meant the seventh day,
You need to reconsider your choice if you own a different way.
"If you love me, keep my commandments"; the Sabbath is one of these,
You need to follow His wishes, if Jesus you're hoping to please.

And even in heaven we'll worship Him upon the Sabbath day,
In honor of God as Creator, our gratitude to display.
And as the years of eternity roll, our joys will know no end,
As we sing His praise and learn the ways of Jesus, our dearest Friend.

God's Time in Stone

The Sabbath day was made for man,
By God's deliberation,
Yet men have managed to change the day,
Without God's authorization.

The Sabbath Day is a special day,
Denoting God as Creator,
To honor any other day,
Implies an adulterator.

You cannot change what God has made,
His law was put in stone.
His law controls the universe,
Belonging to Him alone.

If He had wanted to change the day,
The least that He could do,
Would be to announce this change on earth,
So all would know it was true.

Yet Christ said nothing of such a change,
While here on earth below,
His disciples knew nothing about the change,
You'd think that they would know.

After the early church faded away,
Corruption entered the church.
Men changed the day to honor the sun,
Leaving God's day in the lurch.

It was then that tradition assumed the place,
Of God's original day,
For heathen practices entered the church,
Which hid God's truth away.

God says the Sabbath day is His,
Not Sunday, as men proclaim.
If you choose to worship on other than this,
The purpose of God is defamed.

The Bible makes mention of one day as God's,
It's the seventh day of the week,
If you have a question of which one it is,
Check a calendar as you seek.

The Bible informs us, God's day will be kept,
Not only on earth but in heaven,
If you wish to honor the Creator and King,
God's day isn't just one in seven.

God's Unchangeable Word

On which day should I worship God?
It's a question that all should ask,
To answer this question is critical now,
And involves a significant task.

To study God's Word and follow it well,
Is a challenge that's given to man,
For falling in love with the truth of God's Word,
Is heaven's deliberate plan.

A person must study the Word as it reads,
Without any extra additions,
For there is an enemy working today,
Who deceives with unholy traditions.

The change of the Sabbath to Sunday is one,
That conflicts with the Savior's commands,
For God says, "I change not", and why should He change,
When He wrote them in stone with His hand?

The Lord kept the Sabbath when He was on earth;
At creation, He hallowed the day.
Though choosing a substitute day to observe,
You can't take God's blessing away.

God says, "If you love me, then keep my commands",
His Book does not tell of a change.
When men are observing a day that is new,
They are playing with fire that is strange.

The heathen were people who worshipped the sun,
To accommodate them was the aim.
The church, undertaking this problem at hand,
Introduced a false worship and claim.

Tradition took over and ever since then,
Men have trampled God's Word in the dust,
Neglecting the obvious truth as it reads,
Despising the true and the just.

Christ counseled His men when Jerusalem fell,
They should pray that their flight would not be,
On the Sabbath, confirming the truth that His day,
Would last for eternity.

The Bible goes on to establish God's day,
For in heaven it also will stand,
We're told we will worship each Sabbath there too,
According to God's holy plan.

Though many excuses are offered today,
To observe the first of the week,
There is only one Sabbath the heavens have blessed,
You will find it, if truth you will seek.

The majority won't be successful this time,
No matter how large it may be,
For God is the ultimate Judge in the end,
His commandments are final, you see.

For lying deceptions will come at the end,
Which declare that the false day is true,
And fire will be called down from heaven one day,
In which lies are pedaled anew.

If you're not established in God's Holy Word,
These sensations will surely deceive.
The only escape you will find in that day,
Is in choosing God's Word to believe.

You can opt to ignore it and follow men's rules,
But you won't be in step with God's plan.
It's a matter of whose jurisdiction you choose,
Either God's or those of a man.

For one day when Jesus comes back to the earth,
To gather his children, his own,
The ones who have followed His holy commands
Will be seated with Him on His throne.

Gods of Wood and Stone

The gods of wood and stone are those which neither see nor hear,
They do not comprehend my cry nor see my falling tear.
If made of wood, they can be burned to keep the cold away,
Yet men will bow and pray to them as if to evil, stay.

Though made of plaster or of gold, it doesn't seem to matter,
For they are quickly broken, being useless as they shatter.
They cannot walk, they do not talk, nor can they answer prayer,
For they are only wood and stone, and that is all that's there.

We mock at ancients of the past whose gods were generated,
Because the gods we worship now are more sophisticated.
For one, there is the plasma screen, a time-consuming vice,
And also electronic games and phones with hefty price.

The sports arena, hobbies, and the vehicles we own,
Are things we sometimes worship, and in our hearts enthrone.
The only thing that's worthy of our worship and our praise,
Is He who is Creator and the ancient God of days.

All other gods of wood or stone or any other thing,
Cannot compare with Jesus Christ, our Savior and our King.
Then let us give our worship to the God whose name is love,
Who gives us life and blessings from His throne in heaven above.

Gratitude

Gratitude is an attitude of honest appreciation,
It comes from a heart that has been renewed with godly inspiration.
It views the offering that is made and values the gift and giver,
And praises the effort made by one who took the time to deliver.

For words can be a shallow gift; the action is what counts,
The love that will attend the gift is what is paramount.
A thankfulness for what is done will show a gracious mind,
And often has the tendency men's manners to refine.

For gratitude shows humility in accepting someone's gift,
While being truly appreciative will give the soul a lift.
It acts as water to the plant, which causes it to thrive,
For it takes a little watering to keep a man alive.

Then offer appreciation for the thoughtful acts men do,
If hearts are warmed and fears disarmed, new joy will come to you.
And be especially thankful for salvation that's been won,
By Jesus Christ, the Savior of men, the Father's only Son.

Heavenly Connection

In the beginning, God made the earth as perfect as could be,
He talked with Adam face to face, for he was family.
But after sin had entered in, God's face was hid from man,
So heaven used some other ways to indicate God's plan.

At first, God spoke aloud to them; His form they could not see,
He also sent His Spirit down to guide them carefully.
He spoke His will through messengers, His prophets, brave and bold,
Who wrote the Scriptures down for men: the things that they were told.

God spoke His word through nature's book, showing heaven's love,
Revealing God's desire to bless with tokens from above.
His greatest gift was Jesus Christ, who lived by heaven's plan,
Communicating by His life how we should live as man.

God uses dreams and visions sent to messengers below,
To speak to man of heaven's plan and show the way to go.
He has not left us all alone but speaks in quiet voice,
By guiding us to do His will and giving us a choice.

Do not depend on any man unless God's Word is used,
For some have twisted Scripture texts and thus God's Word abused.
Then open up the Word each day and pray for God to lead,
You'll find the answers that you seek when on His life you feed.

He longs to thus communicate His messages to you,
And if you take Him at His Word, you'll find that He is true.
And then when He has come again and sin has been erased,
Man once again will talk with God in person, face to face.

Hidden Nails

I didn't eat of Eden's fruit which might have come to me,
Nor did I kill my brother when I struck him angrily.
I didn't venture on the roof where David lingered long,
Nor did I hold the coats when Stephen suffered grievous wrong.

I didn't sell my Master for the price that slaves would be,
Nor did I join the heinous crowd to mock unfeelingly,
I didn't hear a rooster crow, the words of Christ to meet,
Nor did I hammer nails into those tender, bleeding feet.

I may not do a thousand things that others may have done,
And yet, when looking close inside, I find a wrong is done.
For in my own deceitful way, I too, have mocked my Lord,
And guilt has rested on my heart and pierced it as a sword.

For selfishness has ruled at times, surprising in its force,
Though I have tried excusing it with alibis, of course.
And yet, when faced with honesty, I find I must admit,
The condemnation that has come has found a perfect fit.

But God stepped in and took my place and died upon my tree,
He took my guilt upon Himself and set this captive free.
In gratefulness, I stand in awe and long to see His face,
That I may thank Him for such love and His forgiving grace.

Hole in the Heart

Not all of the baubles and beads of this world
Can satisfy man's greatest need,
No noble accomplishment, however great,
Is that by which man will succeed.

The hunger that lies in the heart of the soul
Is the need only God can supply,
And by feeding upon heaven's Word every day,
The Scriptures, man's need satisfies.

A man looks for happiness here on the earth
In riches and honor and fame,
He relies on the world's commendation of him
Instead of embracing God's name.

He seeks education and earthly pursuits,
Thinking they will prove adequate goals,
Only to find as he's nearing life's end,
That they cannot render him whole.

The God-planted need that can make men succeed
Is the truth that resides in God's Book,
It will help them find comfort and joy for the mind
If they are but willing to look.

Then open its pages and read for yourself,
Don't depend on the words others say.
You will find in the end, you've discovered a Friend
Who will satisfy needs every day.

Hope for Today

What do you do? What can you say,
When your world has fallen apart?
When the one you love is taken away,
And with him, goes part of your heart?

All of a sudden, the person he was,
And all of the times that you shared,
Come rushing in like a reckless wind,
When you're totally unprepared.

An emptiness comes that can't be replaced,
By another soul around,
For within his thoughtful and caring ways,
A reassurance was found.

Is there a balm in Gilead,
That can comfort the aching soul?
That can soothe and comfort the loss that's felt,
And fill up the empty hole?

Look up, my friend, for a better day
Is promised to those who believe,
For the power of Him who's the Giver of life,
Can all your heartaches relieve.

He is safe in God's hands amd please understand
What God plans to give him in time,
For all of heaven will open to him,
With its mansions and peace sublime.

Then dry your tears, and look to God,
Who has promised His children to save,
For He marks the place where your friend is laid,
While watching over the grave.

And one day soon, and it won't be long,
Till this precious friend you will meet,
As you walk hand in hand in that glorious land,
Casting crowns at the Savior's feet.

Hosea, Prophet of God

Hosea, a prophet of long ago,
Received a strange commission.
He was told by God to marry a whore,
Which seemed a strange position.

The situation was used by God
To teach an object lesson,
When Israel turned her face from God
And lacked sincere confession.

God's tender love conceived a plan
To wake His people up,
For they had worshipped other gods
And then became corrupt.

The prophet was a type of Christ,
The whore was much like us--
God's lost and erring children,
Created from the dust.

Thinking to enrich themselves
By sinful lovers fair,
God's people chose a worldly way,
Which was to them a snare.

Though God had taken special care
To meet their every need,
Yet they had turned their hearts from Him,
Their selfish souls to please.

God hedged His people's way about,
And sought to wall them in,
To steer them from idolatry,
Which was their grievous sin.

In time He wooed them back again,
So they would realize,
That He had always blessed them with
The things they should have prized.

Whenever self gets in the way,
Calamity occurs,
God's way is proved the better way,
Despite what man prefers.

The story shows the magnitude
Of God's redeeming love,
And what He'll do to point the way
And lift man's eyes above.

Hot Off the Press

The current stream of daily news leaves much to be desired,
When facts of what is happening by prejudiced is mired.
The slanderous inferences can give one cause to wonder,
While honesty is swept aside and truth is rent asunder.

For so called "facts" that now appear within the news today,
Are often contradicted when new facts come into play.
It's hard to find the honesty we lived with long ago,
When self-respect and loyalty kept decent men in tow.

The party line predominates and dictates what is shared,
Enlisting those who listen with the prejudice ensnared.
The truth of what is happening is often hard to find,
Unless with intuition one can read between the lines.

You wonder if it's worth your time to watch the news each day,
When rhetoric abounds that strips your confidence away,
It's hard to find an honest man who won't be bought or sold
By political correctness to stand with truth enrolled.

We've come to such a time as this, when honest souls confess
It's time for God to take control and straighten out the mess,
And when He does, He'll rectify the facts and make them straight,
But until then, all one can do is sort them out and wait.

How Can I Know?

How can I know that God loves me at all,
When He isn't around here to see?
And how can I know what the Bible reveals,
Is intended for sinners like me?

Yet when I have opened a Bible to read,
Its words resonate in my soul.
It gives me a peace that before was unknown,
It fills up a dark, vacant hole.

It seems to bring comfort I desperately need,
With a practical sound in its words,
It seems to make sense, breaking down my defense,
In doubting the message I've heard.

When looking around at the world that abounds,
All nature speaks softly to me.
It whispers that Someone much bigger than I,
Is caring for all that I see.

When I look at my life, full of problems and strife,
Full of questions unanswered as yet,
I long for the answers, for quiet and peace,
And would like for some things to forget.

God, I've heard in Your Word that you mean what you say,
That you love even sinners like me,
How these words thrill my soul and give me some hope,
That You true to Your word now will be.

Here's my hand, precious Lord, kind of shaky and small,
For I read that you died just for me,
I've nothing to give, but teach me to live,
And become what you'd have me to be.

Change my heart, clean me up, make me white all inside,
I confess all the wrong I have done.
Don't let go of my hand, but show me Your plan,
As I walk with You now in the Son.

In Heavenly Praise

You hold my life within your hands; my every breath is yours,
You guide each bird in certain flight to home from distant shores.
You hold the spinning earth in tow while hurtling it through space,
Each galaxy and star appears in its appointed place.

The constant beating of the heart is all sustained by You,
You send a guardian angel near to guide in what I do.
If I should stumble on life's way, You send your Spirit strong,
To woo me back to You again when I am doing wrong.

You are the only One in life on whom I can depend,
Though others folks may come and go, you're still my dearest Friend.
Then keep me, Father, close to You, and may I never stray,
And hold me fast within Your arms till we shall meet someday.

How Will You Stand?

How will you stand in earth's last hour
When challenges rise from the dust,
When everything has disappeared
In which you put your trust?

When every earthly friend is gone,
And no one is around,
From whom to draw some sympathy
While you are judgment bound?

If you thought that life was hard back then,
How will you face this hour,
If you have lost connection
To the only One with power?

Now is the time to seek God's face
That all may be well that day,
Under the loving arms of Him
Who can wash your sins away.

For today is the day of salvation,
Not tomorrow, next week, or next year.
Don't loiter or stop to hesitate
When the day of judgment is near.

The rumble of His chariot wheels
Is now the airwaves filling,
Run quickly, God's pardon to realize,
While mercy still is willing.

Surrender your hopes and dreams to God,
His promise will not fail,
He longs to have you come to Him
While mercy still avails.

Although the evil one is here,
He's now a conquered foe,
Though many are deceived by him
Who dwell on earth below.

He holds the power to confuse
By miracles and terror,
Encouraging men to change the truth
To falsehood and to error.

The only way of sure escape
Is found within God's Book,
If you have not uncovered it,
Be sure to take a look.

For God is God, He changes not,
Be sure you understand,
The only way that man succeeds
Is by following His plan.

The judgment then, in God's own words,
Will rule within your favor,
And heaven is the great reward
He plans for you to savor.

Impatience

Do you find that you're impatient; do you find it hard to wait
For things you seem to want right now, which you anticipate?
When you are in the market and the clerk is much too slow,
Does it seem she doesn't understand you have some place to go?

When working towards a worthy goal, which somehow is delayed,
Do you become impatient when you see your project fade?
Impatience is a common thing, which comes to everyone,
We like to find completion in the projects we've begun.

God knows no haste and no delay in plans He has for you,
He wants you to believe that He will help to see you through.
Some people in the Bible had a problem with this trait,
They found it hard to sit around and on the Lord to wait.

When God had promised Abraham a special son to send,
Impatiently, he jumped the gun, the rules of God to bend.
The outcome wasn't very good; it brought a world of grief,
Impatience cost the man a son because of disbelief.

Then Jacob had a problem, too, his birthright to acquire,
By waiting on the Lord, he could have had his heart's desire.
Because he was impatient for the Lord to show the way,
The problems he created there would follow him to stay.

Judas was impatient, too, to see the Master crowned,
He tried to force the Master's hand to bring Him great renown.
Impatience sealed his destiny when he betrayed the Christ,
Too late he found impatience was not worth the awful price.

Impatience can be hard to bear, a fire within to tame,
And yet, it must be overcome to represent God's name.
The answer comes with earnest prayer to overcome this trait,
For no impatient man will ever walk through heaven's gate.

In the Garden

Gethsemane was the decisive place
Where Jesus accepted the cross,
For He poured out His soul in Gethsemane cold,
While wrestling with infinite cost.

From heaven He came to save sinful man,
Well knowing what He must endure,
Yet He shrank from the weight of sin He would bear
Because of a heart that was pure.

He felt the ingratitude rising from man,
Despite all the good He had done,
The long hours of prayer, the healing, the food,
Yet few to His side had been won.

The oozing of blood drops appeared on His face
As He knelt on the ground in dismay,
For why should He die for ungrateful men
Who tried to entrap Him all day?

As a man, He longed for sympathy then,
In this hour of anguishing need.
Though He asked His disciples to watch with Him there,
His words they neglected to heed.

He knew He could choose to return any time
To the home He had left behind.
He could leave mankind to their destiny
Because they would choose to be blind.

Christ wasn't compelled to go to the cross,
Though others might not have a choice,
But because of their sin, men depended on Him,
For mankind had lost its own voice.

Though He struggled alone, His character shone
When deciding the cross was the place,
Where dying, He'd win against Satan and sin,
While He salvaged the whole human race.

Oh, Gethsemane, how you humble me!
Let my tears flow in sympathy here,
Hallelujah to Jesus! for what He has done,
In conquering sin, death, and fear.

Though all turn away from the marvelous gift
For humanity, which He has wrought,
In gratitude now, in submission I bow,
Because of the joy He has brought.

In the Loop

In political correctness, one must cater to the world,
No matter if it's wrong or if it's right.
Somehow, a man's conviction doesn't seem to carry weight,
And the notion is to keep the lips sealed tight.

In church, it's much the same, and if one should dare to speak
And refute the notions favored by the group,
Though the group may seem polite, he'll be banished out of sight,
Being silenced, kept in tow, outside the loop.

It's not supposed to happen in a group that's been informed
Of the values and the truths that one should hold,
But if popular opinion should decide to overrule,
One may find himself outside the cherished fold.

No matter if God's counsel is as plain as it can be,
When the group in power casts the truth aside,
There's little you can do but get on your knees and pray
That the truth will in the future be their guide.

Though truth is rarely popular, and one may pay a price,
For speaking truth in church or in the world,
It's never right to compromise when truth is on the line,
But let the glorious light of God unfurl.

In the Shadow of the Cross

In the shadow of the cross, conviction blooms and thrives,
Transforming cold and stubborn hearts and changing selfish lives.
It softens hearts that cherish sin and points out where they fail,
To do the better things required where love and peace prevail.

The goodness there revealed in Christ, no soul can now resist,
A nagging conscience presses home the truth that will persist.
It was for you He suffered long, both in the mind and soul,
That He might bring about the change which now can make you whole.

Don't turn away, conviction pleads, for you He gave His all,
Be quick to now surrender to His loving, waiting call.
Tomorrow may not come again; this day may be your last,
Reach out and let Him touch you now and stay within His clasp.

Inclusion

A problem arose between Gentiles and Jews,
Which centered on circumcision.
The Jews were confused in what they should do,
Reluctant to make a decision.

The problem descended when Gentiles arrived,
Believing on Jesus Christ,
The Jews thought that they should be circumcised,
No other way would suffice.

Circumcision had always belonged to the Jew,
To banish it seemed to be odd.
They forgot Father Abraham only believed
And was counted as righteous by God.

The real circumcision occurs in the heart,
When the soul completely surrenders.
The outward compliance was only a sign
That encouraged one's faith to engender.

The Spirit had shown God's acceptance for all,
By falling on Gentiles as well.
Ceremonial rituals were left at the cross,
But their memory, the Jews couldn't quell.

They argued, contending these rituals were right,
Reluctant to throw them away,
At Jerusalem's Council, they kicked it around,
Till James rose to salvage the day.

With the Spirit's approval, they moved to dismiss
The need to retain circumcision.
When Christ brought in grace, it then would erase
The need for outward provision.

Most of the ritual laws of the Jews
Were banished by Christ at the cross,
They pointed to Jesus and what He would do,
And after He died, they were lost.

The Ten Commandments will last till the end,
For they were all written in stone.
God's law is a transcript of all that He is,
And so the law stands on its own.

This law is not only prescribed for the earth,
But rules up in heaven as well,
For its principles rest on God's justice and love,
The problems of evil to quell.

The issue was settled, the Gentiles rejoiced,
For Christ gave His life for all men,
This inclusion exhibits the spirit of Christ,
For it always makes room for a friend.

No matter the color of folks or their age,
Their language, religion, or creed,
We're called to embrace the whole human race,
For all are of Adam's seed.

Inequity

A nation of hypocrisy, we quickly fill the street,
With loud and angry protests, injustice to defeat.
And yet, we blink at those who murder unborn babes at will,
Excusing it as normal, a convenience to fulfill.

How dare we feel so justified defending special ones,
When thousands, slaughtered mindlessly, will never see the sun?
We reel in horror at the scene of murder in our land,
Yet who defends the children now who cannot walk or stand?

We gasp at pagans who once gave their children to the fire,
Because they thought the sacrifice was what their gods desired.
Yet our excuse is more than lame: convenience is the goal.
Our pleasure is the highest value that we seem to hold.

Can one support a slaughter house when murder is the plan?
No wonder population has been dropping in the land.
Priority is pushed aside; we honor whom we will,
While those who cannot protest now, we're justified to kill.

Injustice must be viewed as wrong, no matter who's involved.
Until we judge impartially, the problem can't be solved.
It's time to right the grievous wrongs, so that the goal is clear,
Each life is deemed a gift from God and should be held as dear.

Interface

Sin is not just things we do; sin is what we are,
When will we acknowledge that our sin has left a scar?
We're damaged goods; our righteousness is like a menstrual rag,
With nothing to commend us now, on nothing we can brag.

Left to self, we die alone; this goes for me and you,
No opportunity now exists to earn the credit due.
None is righteous, no, not one; our every act and deed
Is prompted by some selfishness on which our pride may feed.

Oh, wretched, bankrupt, foolish man! How little you do know
How much the God of heaven yearns His love for you to show.
Forget your hopeless, helpless self; surrender at His feet,
It just may be eternally that you may chance to meet.

Introspection

Do you find a nagging question lurking in your soul today,
Which, though you try to banish it, just never goes away?
Have you surrendered to the Lord, or have you kept a place,
In which you can avoid His will, yet still be in His grace?

Do you reassure yourself that everything's okay,
While you're still hanging onto things that lead your soul astray?
For God will not let anything destroy His universe,
For when a sin is held within, it soon becomes a curse.

You know God loves you dearly; you're a child of His design,
He always wants the best for you, for you are on His mind.
This life won't last forever; there's no time to play around,
If you would hope to heaven win and with the saints be found.

It may be that the love of riches lures your soul today,
Or perhaps it's appetite that leads your soul astray.
It might be time you're wasting, which could better now be used,
Or maybe it's the things you watch that have your mind abused.

Perhaps you're holding grudges that are hidden in your heart,
Which rob you of your peace, keeping friends from you apart.
It might be some indulgence, whatever that may be,
That strangles your affections and is loath to set you free.

Whatever seems to hold you, is it really worth the price?
Will the loss of all eternity be worth the sacrifice?
The thing about surrender is that you really cannot lose,
You gain the best of now and then, if heaven you will choose.

So think about tomorrow; don't live for just today,
For this old world of pain and death is soon to pass away.
Then cast your vote with Jesus; He'll keep you to the end,
He'll give you peace unknown before and be your dearest Friend.

Jesus, Son of God

Some say that He was just a man and not the Son of God,
Yet no one ever spoke like Him upon this earthly sod.
His virgin birth was prophesied before He took a breath,
He knew that He had come to earth to give His life in death.

His Father testified of Him by sending out a dove,
Who rested overhead in testimony of His love.
His miracles of healing and His raising of the dead,
Though evidence of holiness, would anger men instead.

His strong rebuke to Pharisees because of pride and greed,
Contrasted with the gentle words He spoke to those in need.
His loving, sure forgiveness to the woman caught in sin,
Bespoke a heart of sympathy and kindliness within.

His resurrection from the dead, His promise to return,
Inspired His followers with hope as fires of torture burned.
And does the heart not soon respond while feeding on His Word?
And is it not the grandest truth that one has ever heard?

The Father spoke it publicly, "This is My only Son",
Creator of the world we know when it was first begun.
By faith we know that it is so, and one day we shall see,
This wondrous Savior, Son of Man, with whom we'll ever be.

Laodicea 2

Laodicea, though we are betrothed, my love,
And the wedding is nearing, I see,
I find you're not ready to take up your vows
To become the bride you must be.

My heart is now aching for you to be near,
The wedding is not far away,
You've lost your first love that was sent from above,
In failing to plan for this day.

Your garments are tainted and stained by the world,
You have soiled the one which I sent,
The purest robe of my own righteousness,
Which I have most joyfully lent.

You've been happy for other garments to wear,
The ones which the world has provided,
The ones which you somehow have thought to be true,
But when seen next to mine are misguided.

I find other interests have taken your time,
You've forgotten the mission I gave.
Though the ones you desire seem innocent now,
In time, they will lead to the grave.

You've forgotten to buy my gold from the fire,
The faith that works through love,
For faith that's lacking the works done for Me
Isn't valued in heaven above.

You neither are hot nor are totally cold,
Yet your love is but lukewarm for me.
It causes some doubts to enter my heart
As your present condition I see.

I'm sure you don't know how needy you are,
You feel you have all that you need.
You aren't aware that your nakedness shows,
For with worldly ideas you've agreed.

What is needed today is my Spirit's display,
The conviction that works in the soul,
The first love that drew you to stand by my side,
Surrender that gives me control.

Your freedom will live in submission you give,
For your fetters will be your great joy,
No coercion abides, for you are my bride,
In our union, there is no alloy.

Then come, for the wedding is nearing today,
Preparations are falling in place,
You must hurry, my bride, to be by my side
And feel my enduring embrace.

As you come, bring others, friend and the foe,
For my wedding embraces them all,
Let them join in the feast from greatest to least,
It's for all who respond to my call.

Laodicea, the Last Church

The church of Laodicea can be found in Revelation,
Described as one who is the farthest from assured salvation.
Her lukewarm state repulses Christ, for she is half committed.
Though thinking she's acceptable, her case is not acquitted.

For she has found it comfortable to stay right in the middle,
While gleaning what the world may hold and giving God but little.
Her lukewarm state is like the water found within her city,
Which, neither hot nor cold, becomes a taste to summon pity.

Deceived by wealth and luxury, she feels no urge to change,
She does not note her nakedness or need to rearrange.
She's blinded by distractions that are taking her away,
From study of the Word of God, much needed every day.

Reluctant to address the ills that lurk within her doors,
She self-assuredly inscribes the Scriptures on her floors.
Within the time of judgment, she sits pompously within,
Assured that God will overlook her lethargy and sin.

Though lacking commendation for the state in which she rests,
If willing, she can turn around and give to God her best.
For God has said if she will change, her fallen state to own,
That she will sit with Him one day upon His sacred throne.

Leadership

Leaders make a difference for either bad or good,
They bless the folks who look to them when leading as they should.
The opposite is true as well, for people are like sheep,
They tend to follow those in charge as if they were asleep.

The role of leadership is grave; the end results will last,
The future will reflect what's done, depending on the past.
If leaders are in tune with God and follow His commands,
Beneficence and peacefulness will come to every man.

The leaders who are indolent, the ones who live for self,
Are not concerned for others, but give heed to lust and wealth.
They do not look for tendencies that lead from God astray,
But unconcerned with right and wrong, they look the other way.

The leader who's responsible will keep a watchful eye,
Correcting ills that harm his flock and giving reasons why.
He will not bend to cherished faults, to creeping compromise,
But will initiate reform that's spiritual and wise.

He will not deal in politics, protecting his position,
But will speak up for what is right, despite the opposition.
For great responsibility devolves on those who lead,
Harsh judgment will be laid on those who fail in time of need.

The leader one should focus on is that of Jesus Christ,
Who would not be deterred by sin, but paid the highest price.
For when the Lord is lifted up, men to His side are drawn,
His legacy, then duplicated, will be carried on.

Each person is a leader to all others who are near,
Be sure your actions stand for truth, and to God's Word adhere.
For all will cast a shadow by their life for wrong or right,
Be sure your leadership reflects God's everlasting light.

Light at the End

What do you do when things go awry
And everything's up in the air?
When you cannot see the answers appear,
And your mind is heavy with care?

It's hard to be still and to patiently wait,
Especially when answers delay,
When the future is hidden and results are unsure,
And relief seems to be far away.

Whoever said life would be easy, it seems,
Never lived on the earth for a spell,
Though life can be pleasant and even superb,
Sometimes it can also be hell.

The only solution that comes into mind
When times such as these may appear,
Is to give them to Christ who can carry the load,
Relieving frustration and fear.

For when you succumb to the cares of this life,
The future can seem dark at best,
The only relief you can find at this time
Is to open God's Word and be blessed.

For He has the answer to all of your cares,
Your troubles, your heartaches, and tears,
Although you are tried, you will find in the end,
The answer in time will appear.

Losing the Lord

While tending to your duties, have you ever lost the Lord?
If so, that is the last thing which a Christian can afford.
For soon, you're feeling empty and may seem to lose direction,
Though you had no intention of a sudden disaffection.

The details of a person's work can occupy his time,
Until it seems devotion hour is then no longer prime.
Though tasks remain that may demand your focus and attention,
You cannot have God's Spirit when devotion's in suspension.

It's best to keep the Savior near, by taking time to pray,
To study, and to ask His help while moving through the day.
The tasks can wait until you take the time for sweet reflection,
Then you will be enlightened by His heavenly direction.

The work that you accomplish then will be the work He planned,
And you will be uplifted for the work that lies at hand.
So put the Savior first and best so He's not lost to you,
That you may bless a needy soul, whatever else you do.

Loyalty

What does it mean to be loyal, my friend?
To be honest clear down to the bone,
To stand for the truth, whatever is right,
Though you often may stand all alone.

It means you must take a good look at the facts,
To discover what's honest and true,
And then you must settle the question for right,
No matter what others may do.

It seldom is easy to stand for the right,
For you'll want to blend in with the crowd,
But you'll find that the current will take you downstream,
If you go against what you have vowed.

You must choose before a crisis may come,
The ground upon which you will stand,
If you wait until mayday arrives at your door,
It will not be a part of your plan.

It surely will come, this serious choice,
And your future is what is at stake,
For when push comes to shove, you will not want your choice,
To turn out to be a mistake.

The way to determine what's right and what's wrong,
Can only be found in God's Word,
For all other sources, though highly acclaimed,
Can often be wrong or absurd.

There are only two ways for the traveler to go,
And you really can't sit on the fence,
You must make up your mind, if peace you would find,
As a comfortable consequence.

Determine today to walk in God's way,
If you want to make life a success,
To champion the right will be your delight,
And you'll find yourself hopeful and blessed.

Minutes to Eternity

Have you thought of getting ready for the final judgment day,
When time on earth is over and this world will pass away?
The earth is waxing ancient, like a garment, tired from use,
Which shows deterioration and the problems of abuse.

The signs of earth compel us to awaken from our sleep,
As tragedies now multiply and life is growing cheap.
A restless mood invades the streets, with fear not far behind,
A hopelessness dissolves our dreams and plays upon the mind.

Each nation rattles sabers, seeking dominance to own,
With threats and higher tariffs, as selfishness is shown.
Each evil man is growing worse till even children fear,
Because they cannot concentrate, suspecting death is near.

This all has been predicted by the prophets of the past,
Who warned us quite repeatedly that only Christ will last.
It's time to get on board today; God's Word will see you through.
It's time to make a u-turn now; eternity is due.

Mary, the Mother

Long hours ensued as the victim was dragged,
From pillar to post to the cross,
When Christ was betrayed and denied by His friends,
The soldiers considered Him lost.

And while He was hanging in bloody array,
Where torture and agony blend,
He committed His mother, who wept by the cross,
To one of His dearest friends.

He arose from the grave two days hence,
But rumors of theft filled the air,
The soldiers were paid to conceal what they saw,
And pretend He was stolen from there.

Then gossip and guessing about Him emerged,
Some believed that He rose; some did not,
Whatever the thinking, the talk was not quelled,
It was something that no one forgot.

After much of the gossip was settling down,
I wonder how Mary was treated,
While some must have offered her comfort and hope,
Still others, the gossip repeated.

And surely, some mocked her regarding His birth,
And scoffed at the way He had died,
For wasn't it only the criminals then,
Who were worthy to be crucified?

In the upper room, forty days hence,
Mary knelt with His followers, praying,
For Jesus had promised His Spirit to send,
His power and might displaying.

Whatever the people might say or do,
She believed what the Savior had said:
That He would arise from His darkened tomb,
To salvage the living and dead.

Though she was His mother, she knew in her heart,
That she was dependent on Him,
To salvage her soul like all others on earth,
Not letting this knowledge grow dim.

Although a sword pierced through her heart that day,
When her son gave His life for all men,
She cherished within her the hope that is ours:
That she surely would see Him again.

Mirror Image

When your heart is encouraged to fill up with pride,
At the wonderful things you have done,
Take a moment, instead, to consider the plight,
Of the heavenly Father's Son.

For humility rose to a whole new height,
When Jesus came down to this earth,
Leaving everything grand on which heaven could stand,
While consenting to lowliest birth.

It was humbling enough to arrive if He came,
With His titles of silver and gold,
Yet He chose to be born in a lowly estate,
Which prophecy early foretold.

For as the Commander of heavenly hosts,
Of adoring angels above,
He willingly left the heavenly courts,
Because of unfathomable love.

And while He was here, He did nothing but good,
For the proud, foolish likes of the race,
He fed them and healed all their physical ills,
And held them with loving embrace.

He was hassled and taunted and held in contempt,
When He claimed of His kinship to God,
But His purity shone and by all men was known,
For He carried no boastful facade.

He was hated and hunted by envious priests,
Who to death, His life would condemn,
He, in trial, kept His peace, and His love did not cease,
For He cherished the meanest of them.

On the cross He is pictured in artwork today,
Clad in covering, modest and fair,
But if truth can be told, from the records of old,
He hung totally naked while there.

If pride is your problem with nose held up high,
Just remember the old, rugged cross,
Where the Master, Creator, the Savior of men,
In humility died for the lost.

God's nature is love, in which pride has no place,
Which was seen in humility there,
And if you will surrender your pride and yourself,
You will mirror His image fair.

No Other Creed

There's nothing like the Bible; there is no other creed,
That's fit to guide a man in life and point out what he needs.
It tells him who he is in life and how he came to be,
It also states what God has planned to be man's destiny.

It shows him what is right from wrong and where his parents fell,
It offers choice of destinies of heaven or of hell.
It shows in depth the reason as to why Christ came to die,
And why He is the only One on whom men can rely.

It gives examples of the men of faith before our time,
And how they chose to worship God and seek His will sublime.
It plainly states God's ten commands to show men how to live,
And that the purpose of our lives is not to get, but give.

The Bible points to God's own day, the seventh of the week,
Of which He says, "Remember", His presence then to seek.
No other creed is given man by which his life to guide,
In which he can fulfill his joy and with his Lord abide.

Its sacred pages offer life to those who will comply,
With what is written on each page and will on it rely.
Then open up the Word of God and pray for Him to lead,
His Spirit then will take control and will your spirit feed.

Not All Roads

"There's a heaven to win and a hell to shun",
Not all roads lead to Rome,
For error is peddled on every side,
No matter where you roam.

We've come to a time when wrong is right,
And right, they say, is wrong.
You need an anchor to steady your ship
That will keep you safe and strong.

We used to keep a Bible in hand
To show us how to live,
But now we legislate the rules
So that wrong we can forgive.

What used to pass for homicide
Is called a woman's right,
Now thousands are killed on every hand
While truth has taken flight.

We've thrown the Bible out of schools,
So truth is vague and blurred,
We're reaping now what we have sown
As gunshots loud are heard.

We're penalizing honest folks
For defending what they believe,
While liberals call the current shots
As heaven and angels grieve.

We've strayed away from truth today
When children we confuse,
By telling them that their gender roles
Is something they can choose.

No wonder society's in a mess,
For God is left behind,
And evil will only wax the worse
When truth we will not find.

It's time to open the Word of God
And honor what's written inside,
Shunning the notions of evil men,
Who are led by sinful pride.

For truth is judged by God's own Word,
No other standard will do.
It's only by this measuring stick
That heaven will come to you.

Not Just One in Seven

The Sabbath is the seventh day on which the Bible stands,
For not just one in seven will fulfill the Lord's commands.
The keeping of the Sunday first derived from pagan use,
When Christian churches compromised the message of God's truth.

At the dawn of God's creation, the seventh day was blessed,
Which then became a symbol of the Lord's eternal rest.
In order to accommodate man's worship of the sun,
The day was changed to Sunday, with this travesty begun.

Although God gave authority, some things on earth to bind,
They must agree with what the Bible states from God's own mind.
For He is God; He changes not, according to His Word,
The fact that He would need to change would seem a thought absurd.

The resurrection as a need to change the day is weak,
For God commanded no such thing if in His Word you seek.
God placed a special blessing in His holy seventh day,
This blessing is reserved for all who follow in God's way.

Obstacles

What obstacle stands between you and God,
From making a full surrender?
Do you find it's a relative, hobby, or pride,
Which Satan attempts to engender?

It's sad to pretend you're a Christian at heart,
And carry the trappings around,
Only to find when the judgment arrives,
That deception inside will abound.

Whatever it is that may stand in your way,
It isn't worth all of the risk,
For although you may think life continues somehow,
You'll find life is short and brisk.

Perhaps you're not even aware how you stand,
Some soul searching needs to take place,
You want to be sure you are right with the Lord,
And have given Him permanent place.

If you dedicate self to God's will and way,
Each morning when day has arrived,
He will bless as you go, and His will you can know,
Defeating each snare that's contrived.

When you are determined to follow His lead,
Whatever He chooses for you,
You'll find that the obstacles vanish and fade,
As you dedicate self anew.

Ominous State of the World

Though we moan and decry the state of the world,
Where tragedies often abound,
If sought, one can understand reasons for them,
If we're honest, some answers are found.

The time has arrived for heaven to work,
For men have forgotten God's law,
So said the prophets because of the things,
That would come on this world, which they saw.

When men fail to follow the dictates of God.
His commands, which are not just suggestions,
They are causing God's Spirit to withdraw from earth,
Leaving man with unanswered questions.

The terrors that follow, the evils that come,
The natural disasters that reign,
Are permitted by God because humankind,
Has treated His law with disdain.

Then Satan takes over; he hates humankind,
For they're made in the image of God.
He is eager to banish all comfort and peace,
That exist on this once noble sod.

Because men have trampled on God's holy day,
In honor of that of the sun,
Because babes are killed by the thousands each day,
God decries all the things man has done.

Men have sanctioned relationships God did forbid,
Saying that which is wrong now is right,
They have sought to remove any presence of God,
In our land, now the devil's delight.

Men are angry inside, they are eager to kill,
They are restless because of their deeds,
They, with reckless abandon, desire their own way
Forgetting the world's present needs.

We shall reap what we sow, and the picture is bad,
When men have rejected the good,
To choose their own way, despising God's day,
And neglecting to do what they should.

Each one has a choice to follow God's voice,
Or be caught in the trap made for man.
He can choose heaven's will to be found with Him still,
When God's judgments have entered the land.

Omnipotent God

Just what God is, I cannot say, but this I understand:
That His eternal interest is His love for every man.
Though owning all the universe-- its galaxies, and stars,
His other-centeredness embraces all we really are.

For though I know not what God is, I know His love for me,
As captured by His willingness to die on Calvary's tree.
I cannot comprehend His time, which never has an end,
But this I know by what He did: He wants to be my friend.

He moves in perfect justice in relationship to man,
He only asks for me to trust when I don't understand.
His ways are far beyond my own, for I am but a child,
And yet He is my Father—strong, dependable, and mild.

His willingness to come and die for someone small as me,
Will be my study through the ages of eternity.
I rest within His loving arms while trusting in His care,
Knowing that His watchful eye goes with me everywhere.

As I surrender to this love, Lord, make me wholly Thine,
And may I bask within the joy of fellowship divine.
And help me conquer selfishness till I am more like Thee,
With other-centered love like Yours to share with folks like me.

On Jerusalem's Crest

As Jesus approached Jerusalem's crest,
And took in a glimpse of His city,
The people beheld a scene in that place,
That was sure to awaken their pity.

The day was far spent, and the temple walls glowed,
With the light of the evening sun,
It summoned emotions, erupting with tears,
From the Savior's heart that was wrung.

The crowd that had gathered with jubilant praise,
Expected that Christ would be king.
They were seeking release from the Romans that day,
Expecting the joys it would bring.

As Jesus accepted the praises they brought,
Unlike what he'd done before,
They ran with excitement as Christ rode the colt,
Waving palm branches high all the more.

As Jesus gazed down at the glorious sight,
Of the temple inscribed to God's name,
He was crushed that the ones He had come there to save,
Would denounce Him and cast on Him blame.

He saw past their shouts of hosannas and praise,
To the cross which He shortly would bear,
Thus, He cried for the loss of the unwilling souls,
Who in time would be filled with despair.

He saw the destruction that shortly would come,
To the city rejecting His love,
Although He was willing to sacrifice all,
By leaving His throne up above.

As groans and loud sobbing escaped from His lips,
His body shook violently there.
Hosannas and praises were suddenly hushed,
As the people stood silent and stared.

The mournful emotion that flowed from His throat,
They were baffled to then understand.
They were slow to embrace all the lessons He taught,
Unwilling to follow His plan.

Their leaders, though sticklers for details of law,
Would not the large picture embrace,
Preferring traditions and cherishing pride,
They rejected God's love and His grace.

I wonder today, though that scene's far away,
If we, too, are rejecting His love,
As we focus on things that are with us today,
Instead of on heaven above.

Perhaps we as well are caught up in our pride,
While cherishing treasures on earth,
By worshipping things that will vanish in time,
Instead of the things of true worth.

God forever will miss those who spurn His appeal,
Who decide to resist His great love.
Don't you be the one to cause Him to groan,
By turning your face from above.

But give of yourself in surrender to Him,
And ask what He'd have you to do.
His tears will be wiped all away in His joy,
Because you've embraced what is true.

Only Jesus

Jesus is the only One who meets the sinner's need,
He's always quick to listen, to hear when sinners plead.
No pastor, priest, or minister is competent to fill,
The personal place within the soul, God's peace to then instill.

No one but Jesus can absolve the guilt that wrings the heart.
Confession heard by Christ alone can cause it to depart.
No other ear is meant to hear the cry of desperation,
No man can be depended on to bring in liberation.

Because there is no other name on whom we can depend,
We need to treasure Christ alone and know Him as a friend.
His name alone can thus commence to point us to salvation,
No ritual of priest or king can give illumination.

Then go to Him and throw yourself upon His loving breast,
Confess your great humanity, and He will offer rest.
All men are equal at the cross; it was for you He died,
It's only through His grace alone that you are justified.

Then lift Him up in all you do and glorify His name,
And live your earthly life below to tell men of His fame.
It's only you and Jesus now; walk humbly and you'll find,
A joy you never knew before by keeping Him in mind.

Our Times

"The world is too much with us," said a poet long ago,
To which I'd say that I agree, but he's not here to know.
In every store where you may go, loud music blasts the ears,
And when the evening news is on, composure disappears.

The homeless walk the streets by day, belongings in their packs,
And then by night, they try to sleep with little on their backs.
Each government with selfishness demands, each one, its way,
As tyranny and evil men in power now hold sway.

Children worry at their schools, concerned if guns are near,
Scarcely focused on their books because of nameless fear.
Racial riots fill the streets as hatred grows each day,
Separating those who should be friends along the way.

Women who have been abused are crying for relief,
Pointing fingers at the men who caused them shame and grief.
Women kill their offspring as the population wanes,
While perversion gains acceptance because of legal gains.

God's Word has now been ostracized by legislative halls,
And still we wonder why God's judgments have begun to fall.
Christians fold their hands in prayer on one day of the week,
And yet they seem reluctant every day for God to seek.

The question posed to all this day is one proposed by God,
For when He comes, will He indeed find faith upon this sod?
The choice is ours, my friend, today; it's time to now awake,
Return to God, surrender all; with Him new promise make.

Pandemonium

The mind just finds it difficult to wrap around some things:
Abandoned kids, the evening news, the tragedy it brings.
Disasters come that threaten folks on each and every side,
Statistics keep on rising till bewilderment abides.

It's hard to comprehend the great destruction that appears,
Until the mind is overwhelmed by things one sees and hears.
Bad news can bring alarm and fear from morning until night,
The only respite one can find is fleeing from its sight.

The heart just tends to sicken by exposure to such things,
Such morbid, wanton tendencies, a melancholy brings.
The answer to dilemmas that would suddenly surround,
Is just to turn one's focus on the look that's upward bound.

There only is one answer to perplexities like these,
And that involves the promise of the coming Prince of Peace.
He comes with righteous equity with justice in His hand,
All evils will be settled then throughout this troubled land.

The wicked will be punished, and all records will be straight,
Elimination will be made of tragedy and hate.
God's children will be ushered into heaven's promised land,
Affliction will not rise again; that is the Father's plan.

Then go with God today; comprehend His sacred Word,
You'll find it holds the grandest news that you have ever heard.
No more will sin develop in this sick and troubled place,
But you will find a refuge in God's loving, warm embrace.

Parable of the King and His Servants

A nobleman planned to organize
A kingdom of his own.
He left his servants at his house
While going to claim his throne.

He left with each some money that day,
In hopes they would invest.
When he returned, a king at last,
They came at his request.

They didn't want him for their king,
But he was in control.
He questioned each to see just how
Their story would unfold.

The first had invested his money with care,
improving his holdings well,
His talents grew to ten times more,
As far as he could tell.

Because the king was pleased with him,
Ten towns to him were given,
And he was placed in charge of them
Because his spirit was driven.

The second servant had also improved
His gift by five times o'er.
The king was pleased to offer him
Five towns for gaining more.

The last one said he had hidden his gift,
Which he thought that he might lose.
He said that he knew the king was hard
And could do what he might choose.

The king was wroth and scolded the man
For not improving his money,
He took the gift away from him,
The results were far from funny.

He gave the money at once to the man
Who had earned ten talents more,
While noting those who improved their gifts
Would gather more than before.

The man who chose to despise his gift
Was killed by the king's command.
Since the king's decision and word was law,
His final judgment would stand.

How are you using your gifts today,
Which the Master now has given?
Are you satisfied to hide them away,
Or are you Spirit driven?

There's joy in using your gifts for Him,
Don't bury them in the ground,
He's promised to make them grow with use,
Then more will come around.

Predestination

Does God predetermine before one is born
If he will be saved or be lost?
And if that's all settled, could there be some way
To possibly make up the cost?

Is predestination a Biblical thing?
is it true that a man has no voice?
For whether he's destined for heaven or hell,
Does he really not have any choice?

As I understand it, the Bible is clear,
God is eager to save every man,
But there are conditions which God does require,
And that is to keep His commands.

God's law is a portrait of what He is like,
And He made us to be just like Him.
In our care for each other and honor for God,
We can't let His message grow dim.

Whosoever will come and will trust and obey
Will be part of His kingdom above,
Each man has a choice in how he will live
In sharing with others God's love.

Yes, God has predestined to save every man,
This provision was made at the cross,
But man is deciding by choices he makes,
As to whether he's saved or he's lost.

Pride Goes Before a Fall

Pride was the agent that caused him to fall,
The most honored angel of God.
When Adam decided to buy Satan's lies,
Pride settled on earth's sacred sod.

Pride is a foe that will lurk in the heart,
While raising its venomous head,
And those who succumb to its poisonous taint,
Will find themselves spiritually dead.

For pride is opposed to God's generous love,
And seeks to put self on the throne.
Its only concern is to glorify self,
Promoting its interests alone.

Nebuchadnezzar, when rising to power as king,
And having much wealth to command,
Would not recognize that he ruled as a gift,
Supplied by God's generous hand.

Yet heaven's great mercy provided events,
To cause him to look up above,
To give him a chance to acknowledge the fact,
That his power came from God in His love.

The truthful relaying of dreams which he had,
Should have stripped him from all of his pride,
But he chose to forget just how helpless he was,
And cherished his glory inside.

After giving the king several chances to change,
And to humble his heart before men,
God gave him a dream which his future revealed,
To try to instruct him again.

Refusing to listen, he patted himself
On the back for the glory he knew,
Until like a beast, he was out in the field,
Having grass upon which he would chew.

Then after he'd spent seven years in the wild,
As a beast, grazing only on grass,
He one day awoke from his pitiful plight,
And his undone condition he grasped.

Now humbled and willing to swallow his pride,
He praised God as earth's rightful King,
For he finally had learned to glorify God,
Which caused heaven's angels to sing.

If you have a talent, possessions, or wealth,
Or whatever you own in the land,
Remember, these all are the offerings of God,
To be used at the Master's command.

To give God the glory should be your life story,
Employing the gifts He has shared,
If used all aright, your days will be bright,
And for heaven, you will be prepared.

Rapture

How beauteous is our lovely God! No words could ever tell
The wondrous virtues that surround that name we know so well.
Such patience and longsuffering with us as mortal men,
Cannot be spoken with the lips or written down with pen.

Such pathos filled His breaking voice, such teardrops wet His face,
For men who in Jerusalem would not His words embrace.
His healing touch in sympathy reached out to those in pain,
His joy did swell for those He healed, with health restored again.

His warm compassion with the souls that sin had led astray,
Convicted hearts, restoring them, and taking guilt away.
With fond delight, He loved the sight of people He had made,
He blessed the little children His disciples had forbade.

And even when He gave rebuke, His voice with tears would break,
His pleading was that men would see the sins they should forsake.
He uttered no complaint when He was nailed upon the tree,
For this He came to salvage man and change his destiny.

Heaven will be cheap enough because my Lord is there,
I cannot wait for His embrace up in that city fair.
To be His child and never want for anything again,
Will be my joy and happiness when Jesus comes again.

Reconciliation

Reconciliation is a hopeful, happy thought,
Implying that correction to a problem can be brought.
It centers on relationships that need a bit of mending,
In which forgiveness and acceptance will require some blending.

In the matter of relationship between our God and man,
A trust was early broken, which forfeited God's plan.
God did not plan that man should fall and eat forbidden fruit,
But disbelief and lack of trust then surfaced at the root.

Yet heaven was not caught off guard; solution was in place,
So God could rescue fallen man and save the human race.
The reconciliation then appeared, which came at fearful price:
The cost required the Savior's life, a painful sacrifice.

God's reconciliation was provided for each man,
But it must be accepted by agreeing to God's plan.
Man must repent and ask forgiveness for His faults and sin,
Then God would give amazing grace and wash the heart within.

God gives to all His followers the charge to do the same:
To reconcile the sinner to the Savior's holy name.
Then peace and joy will conquer over Satan and his sin,
As reconciliation comes from God to change a man within.

Render to Caesar

Challenge comes to everyone to keep the traffic laws,
For all should mind authority and hold the rules in awe.
Although the road is lengthy and you're eager to arrive,
The speeding limits guard your safety when you choose to drive.

Remember, one must render unto Caesar of his own,
Because the God of heaven placed him there upon the throne.
It's not alone to Caesar that you're called into account,
But also to the God in heaven, who is paramount.

Each thoughtful, proven entity has rules by which to live,
When people choose to follow them, they satisfaction give.
When people opt to disregard the laws that are in place,
These folks become a menace to ensnare the human race.

Though sometimes you might break the rules when no one is around,
It's best for one to honor them and stay within their bounds.
The penalty, if one is caught, is hardly worth the cost,
Especially when your purse is emptied and your means are lost.

So if you find it difficult to keep the rules of men,
Remember, laws are set in place because they are your friend.
So use a little discipline when leaving your abode,
Then you can miss those blinking lights and sirens down the road.

Return to the Cross

If you are discouraged and nothing seems right,
And all you have cherished is lost,
When life throws a curve, and you're losing your nerve,
You need to return to the cross.

When confusion surrounds you and people confound you,
And life seems to fill with despair,
It's time to regroup, to settle your nerves,
And come up for much needed air.

When people and objects on which you depend
Disappear, and it seems you're alone,
The Savior is with you to settle your fears
When lacking the things you have known.

Keep your eyes on the cross, for Christ, too, suffered loss,
When He gave up all heaven for you,
And He has a plan to salvage each man,
And from heartache and loss bring you through.

Return to the cross when it's hard to forgive,
For it's there He forgave all your sin.
If He wiped your slate clean, have the grace to forgive
Some person who wronged you within.

The cross is the answer to all of life's ills,
The hatred, the pride, the deceit,
For it's there on the cross Jesus suffered great loss,
That sin might sustain a defeat.

The ground at the cross is level for each,
No matter position or race,
Christ suffered for all that they might receive
His love and most generous grace.

The cross is the place to lose selfish pride,
For Christ hung there naked to save,
That we might embrace something we don't deserve—
Life eternal instead of the grave.

Salvation 102

How perfect do I have to be to meet the Lord's approval?
And can I know I'm justified by sin's complete removal?
I'm called to be as perfect as our Father is in heaven,
And yet my nature seems to be like poison grown in leaven.

I wander and I stagnate in the murky pool of sin,
There is none righteous-no, not one, for none is clean within.
Until I look upon the cross, there is no hope for me,
I feel no inclination to behold eternity.

It's only as I gaze on Christ, I find a higher goal,
I'm drawn by Calvary's perfect love that sinks into my soul.
I see myself for what I am--in filthy rag condition,
In contrast to His perfect life, I bow in deep contrition.

All broken now, I'm lifted up to view His perfect life,
A life unselfish to the core, bereft of human strife.
Instead of rags, He offers me His robe of righteousness,
Reflecting His pure character, with which the world to bless.

He bids me go and sin no more, but then, alas! I fall,
I am embarrassed by my sin, my weakness to recall.
His loving eyes then gaze on me in my undone condition,
He lifts me up, forgiving me, despite my poor position.

In gratitude, I'm strengthened by His kind and loving ways,
I cling to Him and ask Him to be with me all my days.
Though I may not be perfect, yet I know who holds my hand,
He bids me yield to His desires and follow His commands.

I know that I am justified; it happened at the cross,
He paid the price; I am redeemed from my eternal loss.
I see Him now as beautiful; He makes my heart to sing,
I know He's coming soon for me—My Master and my King.

Samson, a Case in Point

Samson is often remembered today,
As being the strongest of men.
Yet he was enslaved by the weakness of flesh,
Which brought on a tragic end.

Women were often a challenge to him,
Along with numerous things,
Which, though he was summoned by heaven to serve,
Were sure to catastrophe bring.

For he was deficient in self-control,
And lacking a healthy restraint.
Though he was admired for excelling in strength,
His moral values were faint.

He wanted whatever he wanted, it seems,
And he had to have it now,
"Get her for me, for she pleases me much,"
Was his thoughtless, wanton vow.

He was wild and untamed, reacting with speed,
When things didn't go his way.
His willful direction would enemies make,
Before the close of the day.

His enemies finally captured the man,
Put his eyes out, and made him a slave.
For his hair had been cut, the source of his strength,
Betrayed by a woman he craved.

Though he didn't quite measure with heavenly plans,
God used him in spite of himself,
When God's in command, He will have the last word,
And will not be put on the shelf.

The foes of Samson were God's as well,
And when his hair had grown back,
Though he had been blinded because of men's wrath,
He recovered the strength that he lacked.

His marvelous strength was a gift from above,
By which God intended to bless,
But because of his juvenile, self-centered ways,
His life had become a sad mess.

When a great celebration was held by his foe,
He was brought in their triumph, to tout.
He was tied between posts in the temple they'd built,
And thus couldn't flee or get out.

Though mocked and derided, yet God had decided,
That Samson could serve a great end.
For when Samson acknowledged mistakes he had made,
He prayed God deliverance would send.

He grabbed the two pillars by which he was bound,
And because his great strength had returned,
He pulled with his might, and the building came down,
When he God's direction discerned.

It's a sad, tragic story that's lacking in glory,
For he died with God's foe and with his.
For if Samson had followed God's plans for his life,
It might not have ended like this.

Yet God is so patient, so loving and kind,
He will often use folks less than whole,
For His fervent desire is to save every man,
Who is willing to give God his soul.

Service with a Smile

It's always pleasant to be served, but when a need appears,
It takes a bit of character to do the work that's near.
The servant is not greater than the Master that he serves,
He will not from a needed task or humble project swerve.

Perhaps no one will notice if he's faithful to these tasks,
And maybe no one who's in charge will even think to ask.
But there is an Observer who will keep a record clear,
By taking note of who is willing when a task is near.

For the modus operandi of heaven is to serve,
And not from any humble task to disappear or swerve.
For angels do God's bidding, serving people here below,
They spend their time in ministry, in running to and fro.

And even God Himself will work by keeping all in place,
The galaxies and planets and each star that moves through space.
The beating heart of every man now rests in His control,
He keeps a watch on every person, whether young or old.

Since God is faithful to His task, should not we do the same,
By serving where there is a need in honor of His name?
If we respond in willingness and serve till day is done,
God's greeting will be music when we hear the words, "Well done!"

Seven Seals of Revelation

The seven seals resemble churches shown in Revelation,
They reinforce the principle that's used in explanation.
They first repeat and then enlarge upon the things of God,
Fulfilling His predictions for those living on earth's sod.

The white horse is a symbol of the apostolic age,
Wherein the gospel spread to men with power to persuade.
The red horse symbolized the time when emperors used their power,
To persecute the Christian faith that bloomed within that hour.

The black horse represents the time when compromise was made,
With gospel truth rejected as traditions did pervade.
The horse of gray exemplified the darkness of the ages,
When men were killed by rack and fire because of papal rages.

The fifth seal represents the time of Luther's Reformation,
When men were persecuted for their "faith in Christ" salvation.
The sixth seal showed predicted signs in sun and stars and moon,
Which then foretold the coming of the Savior would be soon.

The seventh seal is yet to come: arrival of the King,
When skies will fill with angels bright, salvation's song to sing.
For Christ will come as conqueror to take His children home,
Where they will live in peace and joy, no more to ever roam.

The symbols shown within the seals are God's alert to men,
To show that He is still in charge and soon will come again.
Though some may read the messages and never understand,
Yet with the Spirit's guidance, they can contemplate God's plan.

Signs of the Times

People dying by the thousands, no relief in sight,
Floods, tornadoes, fires persist; plague destroys by night.
Politicians criticize and castigate each other,
Ever slow to recognize their foe is still a brother.

Angry protests flood the streets; violence fills the land,
Homes are lost, minds confused, who knows where to stand?
No one seems to be at peace; what is going on?
Blame is cast about at will; sanity seems gone.

Slowly, this has come about: suspicion, hatred, vice,
In turning from God's holy word, men's souls are turned to ice.
As men now trample on God's law, His Spirit will withdraw,
Leaving men to reap their choices, which the prophets saw.

With God's Spirit thus withdrawn, the foe of God steps in,
Promoting chaos in the land and every kind of sin.
Turn back your foot from off God's Word, where it does not belong,
Admit reluctance to obey; confess your sin and wrong.

Stop killing babies, blessing gays, approving what is wrong,
It's time to turn your steps around; don't follow wayward throngs.
For judgment hastens on our land; God's coming will be soon,
Be sure that you are on God's side and to His will attuned.

Solid Ground

If you never stand for something, you'll fall for anything,
Just know the thing you're standing for must have a truthful ring.
Be careful where you choose to stand; not every place is real,
You may have chosen such a place where error is concealed.

The Bible is the only place where it is safe to stand.
All other ground, despite its boast, is set on shifting sand.
Beware editions that were changed from truth which God has said.
Be sure the words as spoken there are from the living Bread.

For some have changed God's words at length to suit their selfish taste,
And by this action, set their feet where evil is embraced.
Don't blindly go where some have gone, where angels fear to tread,
Lest by so doing, you may find its message is but dead.

For God is God, He changes not, don't follow sinful man,
But cling to every word of truth God wrote in His commands.
For by this word, we shall be judged, for God will have His say,
All other words will be destroyed on that great judgment day.

Be sure you're standing on the Rock of Jesus and His Word.
His message is the only one that should be seen and heard.
For if you don't know where you stand, your case will hopeless be,
But choose to stand for what is right and gain eternity.

Solutions

Solutions can turn into problems today,
If not in accord with God's Word.
They can even exacerbate trouble as well,
With results, confused and absurd.

The only solution worth trying is one
That is found in the words of God's book.
If that is not what is considered today,
Then it's time you should take a new look.

Hold fast to that which is written by Him,
God's Word marks the path that is true,
And it's only by heeding its counsel today,
God's Spirit, your life can renew.

For men paint themselves in a corner, it seems,
Then look for a way to escape,
Their answers are not what will solve anything,
But can only the problem, reshape.

They rely on their own human wisdom and thought,
Which never a problem has solved,
Expecting a ready solution to needs,
Which will magically seem to evolve.

Right in front of their nose is the answer that sits
On a shelf that is gathering dust,
Which offers the only solution today
That is worthy of genuine trust.

Get down on your knees with your problem in mind,
And look for the answers inside.
God has promised He'll give you solutions to all,
If you in His Word will abide.

Though answers may never come quickly at once,
God will give you the patience to wait,
The solution will come if you wait upon God,
And His answer you'll celebrate.

Star Struck

When I behold the stars at night, how small I seem to be,
Their massive span across the sky just seems to humble me.
Their patterns, unexplainable, intrigue imagination,
Of why they are the way they are, in all of God's creation.

The blackness of the night reveals the magic of their glow,
Compared to all their majesty, I shrink in size below.
And why do shooting stars go by? What causes them to fly?
What purpose do they serve at all? These answers are denied.

I only know when I have gazed on all that's present there,
That I am overwhelmed, it seems, with all their beauty rare.
How great must be the universe, more than the eye can see,
What wonders God has kept in store to share with you and me.

Stewardship

A steward is one whose assignment is this:
To care for his master's possessions.
If he is not faithful with what he is given,
It's more than a slight indiscretion.

As Christians, it's more than just turning in tithe,
That's the least that a person can do,
For all that we have and all that we are,
We owe to the God who is true.

It is He who has made us and not we ourselves,
Every breath that we take comes from Him,
He keeps our hearts pumping, renewing our strength,
He monitors organ and limb.

We owe Him, not just for the means that we have,
But for every endowment and gift.
These treasures are loaned so that they can be shared,
With others to give folks a lift.

Our talents and influence come as a trust,
To use at the Master's command,
These gifts are a loan, and the way that they're used,
Will soon be required at His hand.

God's Word is a trust to His people as well,
We should study so we are approved.
We mustn't subtract or add to His Words,
His commandments cannot be removed.

We must give an account for the use of our time,
Improving the moments of life,
Doing for others the things that they need,
Avoiding disruption and strife.

For God does not live for Himself, we will find,
He sustains all the worlds in their place,
And He wants us to catch of His Spirit today,
As we share of His wonderful grace.

Surrender

What exists in your life today that keeps you from surrender,
To God who gives you life and breath and is your soul's Defender?
The way that you relate to Him will matter in the end,
He knows the thing that's best for you, for He is your dearest Friend.

Could it be your job or friends at work have drawn you from Him now,
Or is it a loved one close to you that's become an excuse somehow?
Could it be the lifestyle that you live, or maybe a cherished sin,
Which keeps you from full surrender to the little voice within?

Is it ambition for money or fame, or desire to do your own thing,
That stops you from embracing God and to your will to cling?
If you should love another on earth more than Jesus, your Friend,
You won't be worthy of Him who died to save you in the end.

Whatever the matter or person that tends to steal your heart away,
You need to keep perspective close as you live your life today,
For in time, when all is said and done, and heaven's gates swing wide,
It's those who fully surrender to God who will find themselves inside.

Testing Time

To those who know to do what is right,
And choose to do wrong, it is sin.
For God up in heaven will never be mocked,
No matter your color of skin.

You may not be stricken with lightning or fire,
The moment you choose to do wrong,
But you are still dealing with God up above,
Who has proven Himself to be strong.

Although God is patient and eager to save,
He never will parley with sin,
And those who presume on His mercy in time,
Will discover the mess they are in.

God says what He means and means what He says,
In the Bible He left for us here.
He has stated His will for the things we should do,
Making everything perfectly clear.

We can choose to neglect to study God's Word,
Yet He holds us responsible still.
What He asks us to do is the best for us, too,
And is easy enough to fulfill.

We must honor the Scriptures, believing the truth,
Not accepting the changes of men.
We must reverence His Word, not things we have heard,
For God will be Judge in the end.

If you find you have strayed from God's will and His way,
And desire in His will to be found,
Right now is the time God has given to you,
To repent and to turn things around.

You will find there is joy in doing His will,
In the knowledge of doing what's right.
If you give Him your heart and make a new start,
Your sleep will be peaceful tonight.

Test of Truth

To testimony and the law as written in God's book,
We're told to give more earnest heed and take a deeper look,
For herein do we test beliefs that come from every man,
To see if they have been derived from heaven's holy plan.

For so-called truth must always stand the scrutiny of God,
As written and as practiced by God's Son when on earth's sod.
For if beliefs which men may hold oppose God's written Word,
They don't originate from God and never should be heard.

Tradition can be good or bad, depending on its source,
But it must pass the muster which the Scriptures reinforce.
It's always well to keep in mind that evil does exist,
And Satan's ploys are subtle in which error does persist.

For what more subtle method could be enemy derived,
Than that of false religion in which error is contrived.
The holy mantle that is thrown upon such false pretension,
Is never made more holy by elaborate convention.

For God is God, He does not change, let Scriptures be the test,
For only those who live by them will enter heaven's rest.
Do not accept the word of man for what God's Word reveals,
But meditate on Scripture source, for only it is real.

The Absence of Time

Because there is a beginning,
We assume that there must be an end.
All things we observe on this planet,
Encourage this message to send.

Each day commences with morning,
And ends with the darkness of night.
The seasons begin and they vanish.
The stars come and go with their light.

A man who is born in the morning,
Will eventually take his last breath.
His birth is a joyous beginning,
While sadness accompanies death.

The flowers will come to fruition
And bloom in their radiance bright,
Only to fade in the evening,
Succumbing to darkness of night.

Friends come and they go in a lifetime,
They're here and eventually gone,
Replaced by the life's constant flowing,
By circumstance moving along.

Because we observe a beginning,
We think that there must be an end,
The only exception is Jesus,
Who always and ever has been.

For He has been one with the Father
Where time can admit no beginning.
He was long before earth was created,
Or man was in need of God's winning.

He dwells in the past and the future,
He exists as the great "I AM",
He is part of the heavenly Godhead,
And by destiny's choice, the Lamb.

The love of God has existed
As long as there's been a God,
It's the only thing that is eternal
That exists on this earthly sod.

His selfless life is His glory,
Over time it conquers and towers,
And it's only by heaven's salvation
That the absence of time becomes ours.

The Big Picture

The only right way to evaluate truth
Is to study God's Word for oneself,
The importance of life will not come into view
If the Bible is left on a shelf.

God's Word will tell you why you are here,
And what you should dare to believe.
The answers are written on every page
So that you will not be deceived.

Our God has a plan for each woman and man,
For He made you with infinite care,
He wants to reveal His design for your life,
So of truth you are fully aware.

Don't lean on your pastor, your cleric, or priest,
But open your Bible and read.
You'll be happy to find you will gain peace of mind
When all of its counsel you heed.

Each page holds a piece of the puzzle enclosed,
And when all of the pieces are found,
They all work together, portraying God's will,
Expressing a truth that's profound.

You cannot depend on the wisdom of man,
Who can manage to twist what is said.
Your only assurance is asking for God
To interpret the words that are read.

Each man has a duty to read for himself,
While asking the Spirit to lead,
For when in the judgment, you stand before God,
Only truth will answer the need.

For only by study will you be approved
And will rightly the truth ascertain,
For when God's glorious kingdom has come,
Your place in His home will remain.

The Death of Reverence

Whatever became of reverence?
The one that we used to know,
In which one entered a worship place,
With voices muted and low.

Where people were hushed in quietude,
For God was in this place,
Where they could feel His Spirit near,
And angels would veil their face.

It's become more vital to check with friends,
That we often find are there,
Than to seek the friendship of our God,
And offer our praise and prayer.

It seems we've forgotten whose presence we're in,
While absorbed in the commonplace,
Forgetting the God who has made the worlds,
And suffered to take our place

Reverence is now an unwelcome word,
It seems to have died on the vine.
It's been swallowed up for friendship's sake,
While reluctant our words to confine.

The music grows loud, we try to compete,
Speaking louder so we may be heard,
Until the room sounds like a marketplace,
Conversations all fuzzy and blurred.

It seems that now, we've forgotten the point,
Of going to church at all,
It's become a social event instead
Of a time on God to call.

We might as well have stayed at home,
A better visiting place.
Than to go to church to mingle and talk,
The honor of God to deface.

And are we not shooting ourselves in the foot,
By pretending to worship the King,
While we go our own way, and speak our own words,
Intent on doing our thing?

It's time to give God our first and our best,
By honoring Him above,
By offering the reverence to which He is due,
As evidence of our love.

The Devil's Tools

The greatest battle that ever was fought,
Began in heaven above,
Where Lucifer, an angel of God,
Contested the Father's love.

By spreading deceitful suggestions around,
He maligned the intentions of God,
He misguided one third of the heavenly host,
Who later were cast to earth's sod.

He was no longer welcome in heaven above,
For he chose not to change or repent,
His deceptions were carried to earth to be used,
Where he and his demons were sent.

The battle on earth isn't fought with a sword,
But is fought in the mind of a man,
Where the devil still plies his deceit as before,
By the use of the tools in his hand.

Power is one irresistible tool,
Which he dangles before human minds,
For it tends to corrupt as position is gained,
Causing men to be selfishly blind.

The second device that he uses is pride,
Which focuses largely on self,
Until a man thinks he is higher than all,
Laying kindness and peace on the shelf.

Presumption is also a powerful tool,
That suggests God will overlook sin,
But God is not mocked when we choose to do wrong,
In hopes He'll excuse it again.

The fourth tool is pleasure, forgetting that life,
Is a challenge, requiring one's best,
For indulgence in worldly amusements and lust,
Will perish with all of the rest.

These four special tools, Satan uses with skill,
Which can topple the very elect,
Unless they have cherished the Scriptures of old,
Not choosing God's words to neglect.

The devil has studied the frail human mind,
For thousands of years in the past,
And it's only by keeping the Scriptures in mind,
That man will see heaven at last.

The Empty Tomb

How unexpected was the scene that met the women's sight,
The morning after tear-filled eyes had passed the weary night.
For as the women lingered near the open, empty tomb,
The scene that met their startled eyes replaced their solemn gloom.

Two angels stood beside the tomb, which heretofore was guarded,
By soldiers keeping watch who then in panic had departed.
The angels, hovering close beside the dark and empty place,
Informed them of the risen Christ who'd conquered death's embrace.

"He is not here; He's risen," came the message to their ears,
As growing hope electrified their minds and banished fears.
Excited then, with joyful hearts, they rushed to tell the rest,
Of what they had experienced and how their hearts were blessed.

That joyful moment was the start of all that matters now,
For with the rising of the Christ, the universe must bow.
His sacrifice has paved the way, redeeming what was lost,
As Satan's death certificate was signed by Jesus' cross.

The weary, lost, and sinful world has found a sure escape,
Christ's sacrifice has closed the yawn of sin's extensive gape.
Rejoice, O heavens, sing with joy! Salvation is secured,
The death of Christ has paid sin's price, and victory is assured.

The Force of Love

The Jews desired their coming King to take the Romans out,
And raise the Jewish banner high, their enemy to rout.
But when Messiah came to earth, He had a different plan,
He breathed another attitude to spread throughout the land.

He said His kingdom wasn't here, or else His men would fight.
He didn't come to start a war, but came to bring the light.
For words of truth came forth from Him as counsel would unfold.
His weaponry was charity--not swords or sabers bold.

A healing touch was in His hand; He catered to the needy,
He minced no words of strong rebuke to patronize the greedy.
He preached His gospel on the hills and from a fishing boat,
And quieted a raging storm to keep some men afloat.

He healed the sick, the lame, the blind, with just a simple touch,
He even brought the dead to life, now rescued from its clutch.
Because He was not violent, but humble, pure, and kind,
He wasn't the Deliverer they featured in their mind.

His mode of operation was of love and not of force,
Because of that, they set about to criticize His course.
Jealous of His following, their anger knew no end,
Until it festered into hate, in which death would descend.

The use of force is not God's plan; He uses love to win.
He shares with men His gracious heart to coax them not to sin.
He proves Himself a gentleman by giving men a choice,
And though He's kind and patient, He will have the final voice.

The Forgotten Commandment

Why are folks so hesitant to keep God's ten commands,
When everybody knows it is the law on which God stands?
They claim that they believe the Bible is God's exceptional Word,
And yet, by actions otherwise, you think they'd never heard.

Most folks profess to keep God's law, and yet, at one they blink,
The one that says, "Remember" should make them stop and think.
They keep the nine agreeably, but cast the one away,
As if it wasn't meaningful to keep God's Sabbath day.

Men tried to change the Sabbath day in honor of the sun,
What made them think they had the right to do what they have done?
Because men changed it years ago, it's now become tradition,
And men today continue in this spurious position.

Men had no right to change God's day, no matter what the reason,
The fact that they have gone ahead amounts to outright treason.
God states that if you love Him, you will keep all His commands,
By breaking one, you've broken all, and that is where it stands.

The law is but a transcript of God's character, we're told,
He doesn't change, nor does His law, which all should now uphold.
Whom will you choose? The God above, or sinful, fickle man?
It's up to each to make a choice; be careful where you stand.

The Forgotten Day

The day God said to "Remember",
Men have opted to forget,
Replacing it with a different one,
But the war is not over yet.

The Sabbath was made for man,
It wasn't just for the Jew,
But they were entrusted to share this truth
With others like me and you.

The Sabbath is the special sign
Of God's supreme creation.
It points to Him as Creator of all,
The Lord of every nation.

He set it apart as a special day
For man to turn to Him,
To worship and to pray in awe,
And let the world grow dim.

Though a person needs to honor God
On every day of the week,
The seventh day was set apart
On which our God to seek.

God blessed the day and hallowed it
From any other day,
It was a time to leave one's cares
And spend some time to pray.

The attempt of men to change God's day
To another day is wrong.
Whatever excuses men may give,
The first day doesn't belong.

For God is God, He changes not.
He says so in His book,
If you desire to know what's right,
Then take another look.

In keeping Sunday, men are deceived,
For it's not in God's commands.
In breaking one, you've broken them all.
It's a shaky place to stand.

No man has been given the right on earth,
A different doctrine to find,
For whatever men do, must always be true
To what God had in mind.

God said not a dot of the law must be changed,
For it represents His will,
And when Christ was here, He kept God's day,
And we should keep it still.

The controversy rages on,
Whose authority will you exalt?
Will it be God's or sinful men's?
In one there remains a fault.

Then check it out; don't take my word,
For the truth appears in God's book.
No change is spoken of Sabbath there,
This fact you will find if you look.

But after Christ had come and gone,
The early church wandered away,
Adopting the pagan rites of men,
And attempting to change God's day.

For during the time of the papacy,
Although God's truth had been given,
It was kept from the common people at large,
By Satanic influence driven.

The truth was supplanted by pagan rites
And many a false tradition,
While men sank lower in hopelessness,
Which worsened their condition.

After thousands of years of being denied,
The light of truth was found.
When the printing press came, many wrongs were named,
And minds were then unbound.

A needed cry escaped from those
Who were tired of the church's oppression.
The truth of the Sabbath, long kept out of sight,
Emerged from dark suppression.

All through the years, God protected His truth
Where faithful men were found,
Preserved from ire of the papal church,
Wherein the conscience was bound.

The truth of the Sabbath shines brightly today.
On what side will you stand?
For oppression once more will rise again
In this once favored, promised land.

"We ought to obey God rather than men",
If the two should disagree,
For by doing so, we honor God,
For He is our liberty.

You cannot force the conscience of men
And stay in the favor of God,
For truth will conquer in the end
On earth where God has trod.

The showdown is coming soon, my friend,
Whose authority will you choose?
Will you stand for the holy Sabbath of God,
Or watch heaven's Word abused?

The end is near; that should be clear
From events we see at the door.
Determine today to walk in God's way,
Be sure that the truth you adore.

The Gold Standard

The object by which wealth is measured today
Is said to be that of gold,
Yet God has a Golden Standard as well,
Which existed from ages of old.

The standard of God resides in His words
That He wrote on tablets of stone,
These principles guide both heaven and earth,
And belong to God alone.

The Golden Standard that judges men
Is the Ten Commandments God gave,
It was given to guide all men to Him,
From their birth right down to the grave.

Because it's a transcript of Who God is,
It never can be rearranged,
And woe to those who have taken the task
To attempt its words to change.

For God is God; He does not change
To suit the fancy of men,
And those who would think to take Him on
Can never their course defend.

Then weigh your thoughts and words and deeds,
By this, you will be judged,
For it will not go well for you
If its principles you have begrudged.

This Standard of Gold will never grow old,
For its Maker is God above,
Who has given these rules as a blessing to men
Because of His infinite love.

Then place its principles down in your heart,
And let them direct what you do,
In comfort and peace you must do God's will,
His blessings are meant for you.

The Greatest Battle

As a Christian, one knows there are battles to fight,
But the biggest engagement is self,
For man has propensities yet undisclosed
Which lean towards position or wealth.

Man wants to be noticed or longs for ease,
With comforts that money can buy,
But it isn't in self to place on the shelf,
The things that he ought to deny.

The battle is present and ever survives
To harass, to plague, and to plead,
And the best of man's efforts are never enough
To cause him to win or succeed.

He struggles within, for self bends to sin,
When refusing to look to His God.
And the most he can ever expect in this life
Is to breathe and to die on this sod.

Though the world offers joy in comfort and drink,
And in riotous living beside,
These pleasures won't last because they emit
From a self-centered longing inside.

The God-given need to connect with the creed
That God has provided from heaven,
Is the thing that will bring satisfaction to men,
Causing joy to expand like leaven.

With surrender to God, true humility comes,
With love for sister and brother,
The enticement with self is placed on the shelf
By genuine care for another.

The struggles with self diminish each day
As new goals replace what was granted,
Then joys will evolve as man's problems are solved
As seeds of new life are implanted.

Though the battle with self will always exist,
We can find sure relief from its power,
Surrendering all that we have and we are,
Provides greater strength for the hour.

When the Spirit of God comes into our lives,
We surrender to God's better plan,
For God has a place in which souls will rejoice
In serving at Jesus' command.

The Greener Grass

Why is it that we, as human folks,
Will tend to envy another,
When we could be more charitable,
Considering each as a brother?

Instead of valuing what we have,
We seem to long for more,
We rarely seem to appreciate,
What we already have in store.

We envied the woman who had the eyes,
In the loveliest shade of blue,
Until we found that she was blind,
And darkness was all that she knew.

We thought the man who lived next door,
Was richer than a king,
Until he mentioned he'd lost a son,
For which he'd give everything.

We looked down our nose at the unkempt clothes,
Of the man who lived on the street,
Till finding he carried a purple heart,
But with stress disorder would meet.

We envied the shy Diana of Wales,
Who was destined to have it all,
Until her prince, another embraced,
Which led to her tragic fall.

The various stars of Hollywood fame
Will shine like those in the sky,
Until in the fast-paced life they live,
They will turn to drugs and die.

We long for beauty and wealth and fame,
And hope to travel afar,
While never pausing to realize,
The wonderful things that are.

If we are blessed with a beating heart,
And can view each new tomorrow,
Why should we long for things not ours,
And thus, more troubles borrow?

We need to take stock of what we have,
And value our life anew,
For an attitude of gratitude,
Is destined to see us through.

The life we take for granted,
Is the life we should embrace.
Our friends, our home, our family,
The God who lends us grace.

Since each of us is one of a kind,
We should value the person we are,
Fulfilling the purpose God has for us,
To shine for Him like a star.

"The Hound of Heaven" Revisited

The hound of heaven appears to me,
As an irreverent term for God to be.
The term seems to fit, for God will pursue,
The wayward directions of me and of you.

Perhaps a more fitting term could be found,
Than comparing the Savior above to a hound.
It seems most demeaning and quite sacrilegious,
There surely must be a term more prodigious.

If I knew that a hound had been chasing me,
I'd be running for fright, not for choice, you see.
The analogy seems to be limited here,
For the Savior's pursuing does not include fear.

For He woos us and draws us in kindness and care,
While His love stops us short in our tracks of despair.
He's patient and humble and seldom aggressive,
He offers us freedom, while never possessive.

The thought of a hound as the Lord is absurd,
And it might as well be either deer or a bird.
Perhaps the old poet was getting senile,
By forcing comparison back into style.

Because God is winsome, not sniffing and snorting,
He wins us in time, our habits aborting.
I'd rather choose Him than a hound any day;
You can keep your old hound-- I prefer it my way.

The Joy of Service

Have you discovered the ultimate joy,
Of giving your life away,
Throwing self in the furrow of earth's greatest needs,
And watching what comes into play?

This world is a garden, desiring good seeds,
That will grow into plants that are needed,
The fruit that will blossom can nourish the souls,
Who are feeling morose and defeated.

Each soul is in need of some help on the way,
For challenges always arise,
As people rush madly in haste through life,
Some help is a welcome surprise.

It could be a person is out on his luck,
And needs some assistance today.
His heart will be warmed, his soul will be charmed,
If you choose to go out of your way.

You can render a pat on a weary one's back,
An encouraging word you can give.
Your listening ear will subjugate fear,
And your smile may lend courage to live.

Whatever you have in your hand, you can share,
As the Master has given to you.
Whatever you offer, be sure you're sincere,
And give from a heart that is true.

For the heavenly motto is service, my friend,
All the worlds are sustained by God's hand,
His coming to earth to die for the lost,
Was always a part of His plan.

You can never outgive heaven's Giver today,
But His methods are always in style.
If you copy His ways and give Him the praise,
You'll revel in joy the while.

The Rainbow Promise

The rainbow is a token of a promise made by God,
That He would not resend a worldwide flood upon earth's sod.
For when the ancient men of old were wicked to the core,
God sent a flood, destroying them when He could take no more.

After He had sent the flood, destroying all but eight,
He did not want to worry men or bring about debate.
And thus, He placed the rainbow in the heavens up above,
Which would remind them of His promise, made to them in love.

So when you see a rainbow hanging after storm and rain,
Remember, God is faithful to His promise, which remains.
What God has said, He will fulfill; His promises are true,
And you can put your trust in Him---His promise is for you.

The Last Mission

God's people today are assuredly marked,
The day of confusion draws near,
Each face turns to paleness in dread of that day,
Every heart will be tempted to fear.

As darkness encloses, the enemy hastens,
To turn them from God's Holy Word,
To fear their destruction and make them forget,
The truth they once cherished and heard.

As pagan beliefs rule the day and the hour,
And millions are drawn in the net,
The ones who have studied God's Word and His truth,
Will not His Scriptures forget.

They know that the showdown will finally come,
In the war between Satan and God,
They understand clearly who owns the last word,
As the battle is fought on this sod.

They are captured and gathered for following truth,
Rejected as Christ was by men,
As sheep that are rounded for slaughter they stand,
While hoping to rise once again.

They languish in prisons or huddle in groups,
While bereft of the comforts of life,
They pray without ceasing, release on their minds,
Despising confusion and strife.

Though hungry and weary because of delay,
They remember God's love at the cross,
And how He was willing to die in their stead,
That they could be salvaged from loss.

The truth in God's Word is a bulwark to them,
And nothing can turn them away,
No miracle, healing, or fire from above,
Can turn them and lead them astray.

While days may be dreary and dark be the way,
They know God is good for His word.
Though some may be summoned to give up their lives,
They will not from truth be deterred.

Though fearing that they will be helpless to stand,
They remember that they have been told,
That if the time hastens that they should be killed,
That God will give strength to be bold.

The prisons will fill with the glorious light,
Of angels on missions of love,
They are sent to the saints who have valued God's Word,
As given by heaven above.

They cling to the One who has promised them joy,
In the midst of their suffering and pain,
To the God who has promised them crowns of delight,
When returning His loved ones to claim.

When the heavens shall reel with an earthquake by night,
And the blast of the trumpet rings out,
Those who look for His coming will look up in awe,
As they give a victorious shout.

Though they suffer with Him who has suffered the more,
To save them from infinite loss,
They will know at that moment that heaven is real,
Cheap enough at whatever the cost.

The Law, a Test

The law is a test for heaven to see,
If God's law as written is kept willingly.
Yet after God's law has most clearly been spoken,
Men give little thought as to when it is broken.

God's law is a transcript of all that is fit,
And God does not alter and neither does it.
For all of God's counsels will benefit man,
If he will but live by His heavenly plan.

God's law has been given for man's special good,
And gives satisfaction when once understood.
For God is concerned with the heart and the soul,
If breaking one part, you have broken the whole.

No partial obedience will heaven accept,
For all of God's law must be carefully kept.
It's all about honoring God up above,
For in keeping commandments,we show Him our love.

Men tend to assume that they know what is best,
They keep some commandments and leave out the rest.
They pick and they choose and they find compromise,
Believing they're perfect within heaven's eyes.

But when the great day of God's judgment is here,
They'll find they've neglected God's Word to revere.
No feeble excuse will exempt them to stand,
Because they have chosen to follow a man.

The only safe course is to choose to obey,
And to honor the Lord in His own chosen way.
Tradition and form will not stand in that hour,
To cover for those who neglected God's power.

Then open God's book and accept what you read,
And to every command give a dutiful heed.
You'll find there's a blessing in doing God's will,
Ad that He is eager His truth to instill.

The Rainbow

When seeing colored rainbows hanging brightly in the sky,
Be reminded of the Word of God, on which you can rely.
For His word is always truthful; it's unchanging and it's real,
For God remembers promises, despite what you may feel.

When the earth with water flooded, destroying beast and man,
God wasn't very happy, but He had a ready plan.
With Noah and his family, He would start the earth once more,
He promised not to send a flood as He had done before.

He set a bow up in the clouds with colors He had made,
So that a man, when seeing it, would never be afraid.
Instead, He sent His only Son to salvage what was lost,
Then watched Him die in agony upon the cruel cross.

A rainbow shines above God's throne, a token of His love,
For those of us who dwell on earth who wish to live above.
Then wrap the rainbow 'round your heart and hold it there today,
Knowing when you see it next, God's love is on display.

The Man on the Street and Me

Lord, help me to value the man on the street,
Though smelly and strange he may be,
For as I remember, when I had no home,
You also took notice of me.

For though I was clean, having taken a bath,
You saw the corruption inside,
It was then that You asked me if I would consent,
To let You within me abide.

For what is the difference if men take a bath,
And look all attractive without,
If musings of envy and critical thoughts,
Give reason for God's heart to doubt?

For there is no difference between homeless men,
And those who don't choose to know God,
It may be the homeless is far better off,
Than the white marble tombs on this sod.

For pride and pretension will render men dead,
Though they may be walking around,
It's only when Christ has converted the heart,
That life and new thinking is found.

So let me look past all the dirt and the smell,
To view what you see in the soul,
And help me remember the grace given me,
By helping to make someone whole.

The Priesthood of All Believers

The sanctuary of Biblical times,
Was a pattern of heaven above,
The earthly was made like the heavenly one,
Which God had prepared in His love.

The earthly priest would offer a lamb,
Representing Messiah to come,
Who took the place of the sinner on earth,
Who often to evil succumbed.

When Christ came to earth as the heavenly Lamb,
And the veil of the temple was rent,
The earthly priest was not needed to serve,
For the time of his work was spent.

For Christ at His death became our High Priest,
Who, because of the sacrifice slain,
Became the one Intercessor for man,
In the plan of salvation made plain.

For man could then pray directly to God,
With no one to go in between,
For Christ had opened the way to His side,
A connection that clearly is seen.

The priesthood of all believers is now
A freedom that man can enjoy,
While priests who declare man must reach God by them,
Have become a deceptive ploy.

There is only one God to whom we must bow,
And it isn't a man on the earth,
We can send our petitions directly to God,
The only One seen as of worth.

And those who would try to usurp heaven's fame,
By claiming the powers of God,
Will find they have stolen from God up above,
Bringing judgment to come on earth's sod.

Then send your petitions directly to God,
No middleman need intervene,
The priesthood of all believers is now,
A fact that most clearly is seen.

For all men have sinned while here on the earth,
No matter their robe or their claim,
The only One worthy of worship today is Messiah,
Called Jesus by name.

Reference: Hebrews 7-9

The Principles of Love

What is the essence of love today
Presented in the Bible?
The counsel that's given in Romans by Paul
Has been found to have no rival.

For one, I should think more highly of others,
Much more than I think of myself,
Humility's seen as a quality thing,
In placing pride high on the shelf.

I need to respect another's gifts
And the thing he is able to do.
I need to be impartial to all I meet.
Deferring the honor to you.

I need to rejoice when you rejoice,
And weep when you are sad.
I must never retaliate evil in turn
When my enemy does something bad.

By making an effort to live in peace
With others as well as I can,
I must do my best to get along
With each and every man

I must bless the men who would persecute me
Because of an honest belief.
I shouldn't curse, but bless each one,
Not causing him anguish or grief.

Inviting folks to my home to eat
Ad providing the needs of the saints,
Will be a blessing to them and to me,
If done without a complaint.

I shouldn't let evil distress or dismay,
But should overcome evil with good,
If my enemy's hungry, I will feed him well,
Not returning the evil he would.

The essence of love is to put others first,
As Christ did for you and for me,
In forgetting Himself, He left heaven's courts
To anguish on Calvary.

If tempted to try to put yourself first,
Think of what Christ was willing to do,
For His work was to offer Himself as the Lamb,
Providing salvation for you.

The Quest

From heaven's glorious, perfect place, Christ came for us below,
To face the fierce temptations of a deadly, sinful foe.
The suffering of my Lord and King while dwelling in this place,
Can never quite be understood by those within our race.

For He was hassled day and night by sinister devising,
His life was made a living hell by evil men's surmising.
They pounced upon His every word to condemnation throw,
They filled His perfect heart with anguish we can never know.

They sabotaged His words to tell what they would hear Him say,
So condemnation could be brought to take His life away.
By stealth of word and wickedness and hatred, ill-disguised,
They sent Him to a wretched death, which evil had devised.

True godliness and evil met in battle at the cross,
To wrestle for salvation or the failure of the lost.
Christ went to hell and back that day and won the victory,
He conquered all the horrors of the second death for me.

He felt the final terror that the wicked lost will feel,
Who did not come to Calvary's cross, their sinful souls to yield.
He felt the separation that the desperate souls will know,
When cut off from both God and friend, when God becomes the foe.

Then ponder, friend, this mystery: the love of heaven's Gift,
And let its pathos break your heart and give your soul a lift.
With thankfulness and gratitude, surrender to God's grace,
Extended to you personally and to the human race.

The Reckoning

"Can a woman forget her sucking child? It's sad to say, but true,
For many have forgotten that great worth to life is due.
Though government may grant the right to murder, it is wrong,
A sadness and regret occurs, replacing joy and song.

No inconvenience or expense or judgment gone awry,
Can justify the snuffing out of life to satisfy.
The blood of that forsaken soul will cry out from the ground,
And will be laid on men with whom consent to kill was found.

The one who kills a pregnant girl in our society,
Is called in question of two lives as double jeopardy.
And yet, a woman has the right to kill her child at will,
Such judgment seems hypocrisy with justice unfulfilled.

The person bringing pressure to bear, encouraging one to abort,
Becomes an accomplice to the crime in light of heaven's court.
Though there are cases dubious, regarding the life of a child,
It's better to go with saving a life, than with murder to reconcile.

A woman's choice must always come before she climbs in bed,
Not after the fact, when life is formed, to love, not kill, instead.
Though God is eager to forgive, repentance is required,
As well as turning away from vice, with all such acts retired.

When comes the day when Christ returns and He inquires of thee,
"Where is thy flock, thy beautiful flock?" What will the answer be?
For every life is formed by God within the mother's womb,
Don't be the one responsible for making it a tomb.

The Revelation of Jesus Christ

When John was banished to an isle, surrounded by the sea,
The emperor thought for sure John's preaching would no longer be.
But he had underestimated things which God could do,
And just what would become of it, Domician had no clue.

The Book of Revelation is a message sent from God,
It covers the time after Jesus died to the end of life on this sod.
It's a revelation of Jesus Christ and what the future will hold,
Symbolic language is often used to share God's message bold.

In approximately AD 96, when John was an elderly man,
God gave him a message in symbols and signs, revealing future plans.
It includes a final appeal within to those who have gone astray,
Encouraging them to return to God before the judgment day.

The Book of Daniel offers a clue in understanding John's book,
For symbols occur in it as well, if one will take a look.
Things in the New are based on the Old; they fit like hand and glove.
For both reveal God's will and way and reveal the Savior's love.

If both are studied carefully, you will find they are much the same,
For both reveal historic events and make the future plain.
If you prayerfully study the two of them to see their message clear,
You'll discover God has a master plan; the future is nothing to fear.

The Seven Churches

The seven churches seen within the Book of Revelation,
Depict a solemn glance into the plan for man's salvation.
They represent the churches that lived past the time of Christ
And then continued to the end to carry God's advice.

Though letters John would write to each had current applications,
The counsel that they carried can apply to generations.
For John addressed the state of each-- the good things and the bad,
Correction to each church was sent, with gifts that might be had.

Though some had commendation, they were counseled to repent,
For some had left the love they had and were on evil bent.
While those who suffered for their faith while in the hands of men,
Were told to keep the faith when tried, to win life at the end.

The message speaks to us today if we will take a look,
Regarding how we measure up to standards in God's book.
We need to search our hearts today and let the truth apply,
The admonition speaks to us; its words we can't deny.

These messages will give a glance into the heart of God,
With His desire to woo the church upon this earthly sod.
He wants each one to be prepared for when He comes to call,
He does not want to give us up; He wants to save us all.

The Seven Last Plagues

When Jesus stands up in the temple above,
To declare all is finished and done,
All judgment is settled, all choices are made,
And havoc will just have begun.

The seven last plagues are a judgment of God,
Reserved for those folks who rebel,
Unmingled with mercy, unlike the first ones,
Upon the Egyptians that fell.

The men who have hardened their hearts against God,
Refusing His mercy and love,
Will then feel God's judgments in form of the plagues,
Which issue from heaven above.

The men who have chosen to worship the beast,
Receiving his mark and his name,
Will find they've neglected the truth in God's Word,
And have only themselves to blame.

The plagues turn the water to blood in the streams,
The sun scorches men with its heat,
The plague of the sores only hardens men's hearts,
And sets up their minds for defeat.

This spiritual battle includes all the earth,
And each one will make his decision,
While those who have chosen to follow God's truth,
Will be met with disgust and derision.

But during this time, after Michael stands up,
The victorious saints are protected,
They have fortified minds by obeying God's Word,
And no sins in their lives are detected.

When the fifth plague strikes the seat of the beast,
The civil and secular powers,
Who supported the beast will find it inept,
And withdraw their support in those hours.

The last great deception of Satan will be,
To cause fire to come from above,
He will cause lying wonders and miracles too,
In an effort, pretending to love.

All of this will make way for the "kings of the east",
The coming of Christ and His host:
The legions of angels who fly from above,
In a scene only heaven can boast.

Get ready! Get ready! Avoid all the plagues,
For God has the last word to say,
Accept His salvation and study His Word,
Don't buy men's traditions today.

There's a heaven to win and a hell to be shunned,
Be sure that you're on the right track,
For it cannot be long till the judgment will close,
And Jesus will shortly come back.

The Story of Achan

Before the battle of Jericho came,
The Israelite soldiers were warned,
That they should not take any spoils from that place,
But Achan, God's counsel would scorn.

He kept for himself bits of silver and gold,
And a garment attractive and fine,
He hid them carefully inside his tent,
So no one would know his design.

He thought all was well till the next battle came,
But God could not give them success,
For someone had taken some previous spoils,
And needed to come and confess.

But Achan was slow, his mistake to admit,
So he waited till lots had been cast,
He should have come forward, his sin to admit,
But he waited too late till the last.

God's judgment was swift and complete on that day,
As a lesson to all was expressed:
It's better to own up to what you have done,
To acknowledge your sin and confess.

The time to take care of your sins is today,
It's better to deal with them now,
For if you confess them, the Lord will forgive,
He's promised to save you somehow.

God says what He means and means what He says,
And He never will tolerate sin,
He offers a way of escape for each man,
For there is a heaven to win.

Then go to Him now, He says He will cast,
All your sins in the depths of the sea,
And you will find joy in your service for Him
As you live for eternity.

The True Temple

When the Jewish temple was being built,
It came to a sudden halt,
So twenty years later when Haggai came,
He dealt with the grievous fault.

"While the temple lies in ruins," he said,
"You dwell in your houses fair,
No wonder the Lord cannot bless you now,
For you act like you really don't care."

The Lord stirred their spirits to build His house,
While Zerubbabal tried to lead out,
Though problems arose, they muddled on through,
But when finished, none gave out a shout.

Although the temple was finished and done,
With the first one, it couldn't compare,
For Solomon's temple outshone it by far,
With all its accoutrements there.

Yet God had remarked of this temple new,
"I will fill this place with my glory,"
And in it, all nations of earth would be blessed,
As part of Israel's story.

For it wasn't the building that would make Israel great,
But Messiah would walk in its halls,
He would bring the glory of heaven to all,
Who would answer His passionate calls.

In the new earth, we're told that no temple will be,
For Christ is its temple so fair,
He excels any building that one could erect,
And He'll dwell with His people there.

For although earthly temples were needed below,
The true one is Jesus, our Friend,
With whom we will worship with unrestrained joy,
In that city where time has no end.

The Upward Look

Some things in this life may look scary,
Yet you'll find when it's all said and done,
You'll discover the thing wasn't bad as it seemed,
And your worries have robbed you of fun.

As humans, we tend to be anxious,
We stress over what comes to mind,
We dwell on the worst that might happen to us,
Which robs us of peace we should find.

We tend to forget there is joy
By giving the days of our life,
To the God who has promised that He has a plan,
To save us from heartaches and strife.

Then rest in His love and just trust Him,
He will give you the joys of your heart,
He'll relieve all your stress; in His Word you can rest,
He will make all your worries depart.

The Truth About Miracles

In a place not far from Nazareth town,
In Cana of Galilee,
A wedding there would be taking place,
In Mary's family.

Jesus and His disciples were there,
Among the invited guests,
The hopeful heart of Mary, it seems,
Could not let her eagerness rest.

She sought an occasion to rise that day,
In which Jesus' glory would shine,
Wherein He could demonstrate evident truth,
Of God-given power divine.

Near the end of the feast, it was suddenly found,
The supply of the grape juice was gone,
Mary grasped the occasion for which she had hoped,
Urging Jesus to carry it on.

To honor her motherly faith in His work,
And to strengthen disciples as well,
He proceeded to turn the water to wine,
Which then would divinity tell.

The word spread around, but then it was found,
He had quietly slipped away,
But the word of His act would be broadcast to all,
As a miracle offered that day.

His disciples would meet opposition, Christ knew,
From the leaders who should have believed,
The miracles done were to strengthen their faith,
By the evidence they had received.

Though a miracle serves to strengthen one's faith,
It is best to depend on God's Word,
For the devil can also do miracles, too,
When he by ambition is spurred.

If you study God's Word, you won't be deceived,
By the miracles Satan will do,
For what's seen by the eyes can appear in disguise,
Yet God's Word will always be true.

Spend time in the Word, for there's no other way,
To escape the deception around,
God's Word will reveal the things that are real,
For you'll find in His words, truth is found.

The Victory of Grace

Christ in His humanity did not once consent to sin,
Not even by a thought could Satan score a victory win.
Because Christ chose to let the Spirit dwell inside His heart,
He conquered sin, which caused the devil from Him to depart.

United with divinity, He had the power to win,
So we may also conquer in the mastery of sin.
God offers us His nature of a life that is divine,
That through Him, we may live His life and by His victory, shine.

We cannot serve two masters; they will fight till one succeeds,
Our future is determined by the one to which we heed.
We do not need to sin at all, for Christ will give the power,
To meet temptation with His Word, provided for the hour.

The power of choice is given us: the power of the will,
And if we give our hearts to God, His Spirit can us fill.
He'll give us new desires and goals that by Him we may grow,
Until His love and purity is all that we will know.

The Wiser Word

The Wiser Word which should be heard is that of Jesus Christ,
Who earned it by creation and by costly sacrifice.
He made the world and all within by speaking it in place,
And then by His own blood He died to salvage men by grace.

When He commanded, all stood fast in perfect symmetry,
His mighty works are spread abroad for everyone to see.
He spoke commands by which all men could live in joy and peace,
Then wrote them down in stone to show this rule would never cease.

The evil men upon the earth, inspired by selfish pride,
Then sought to twist the Word of God and set it on the side.
They now will choose to thus confuse the state of human gender,
And by it, show the evil source to which they now surrender.

They selfishly will choose to kill a child before its birth,
Discarding it as if it were a thing of little worth.
They set aside God's chosen day in honor of the sun,
Thus honoring the pagan cults by whom it had begun.

They set aside the Christian stones that made our country great,
Which now have left our nation's future up for sad debate.
For what is right is now termed wrong, and what is wrong is right,
No wonder peace and sanity have fled away from sight.

Man's only hope in this our day will cause him to return,
To God's commands that he has tried to cast away and spurn.
For in the end the only words that matter and will stand,
Are those that God has spoken when He gave His Ten Commands.

"Thou God Seest Me"

"Thou God seest Me", no matter when or where,
You carry me upon your heart, for You are always there.
Though I may never see Your face, Your promise I can read,
And it is on Your truthful words that I can always feed.

Though night enclose around me, and I may feel despair,
I cling to You within the dark, assured that You are there.
Safe passage You have offered me when winds and rain assail,
And I can claim Your promises, for they will never fail.

My name is written on Your heart and sealed with drops of red,
I only need to look to You when I am filled with dread.
Because I know You're watching me in life's confusing maze,
I know it's safe to trust in You throughout my earthly days.

For "Thou God seest me", no matter where I roam,
Whether I am far away, or whether I'm at home.
Then let me rest upon Your words while looking up above,
Assured that You are watching me, wrapped safely in Your love.

Touchstone of Truth

What do you hold as a touchstone of truth?
Is it based on words that were said?
Could it be some wisdom your mother passed on,
Or perhaps is it something you read?

You need to examine the source of your truth,
And evaluate why it's of worth.
Is it based on philosophy, culture, or whim,
Those things men value on earth?

Whatever it is, may I offer a thought,
For you to consider today,
So you can be sure, whatever it is,
You will not be going astray.

The only truth which can stand today,
Is the truth that is found in God's Word,
For it was delivered by heaven to you,
No matter what you may have heard.

Since given by God who changes not,
Its wisdom is guaranteed.
He says what He means, and means what He says,
He's faithful in word and deed.

You can take His message of truth to the bank,
The bank of heaven that is,
Where God can fulfill your every need,
For all of the worlds are His.

If you will but study the Word of the Lord,
And believe with all of your heart.
And ask for His Spirit to guide you today,
His promise to you won't depart.

He'll strengthen your life, bringing comfort and peace,
He'll point out the right directions.
You'll find in His Word many blessings for you,
While resting in His affections.

This touchstone of truth will establish your rock,
This place on which you can stand.
For God's Ten Commandments and all of His words,
Are given to every man.

Then place your feet upon this rock,
Don't settle for shifting sand,
Its truth will carry you home at last,
Arriving in heaven's land.

Travel Companion

Whenever you travel away from home.
Be sure to take God with you there,
He'll be right beside you to lead and to guide you,
In answer to your fervent prayer.

Don't ever start out and leave Him behind,
For He wants to assist you each day,
He'll speak to your heart when temptation is near,
And keep you from going astray.

You'll be an example to all that you meet,
If you model His words in your life,
You can spread heaven's cheer to all who are near,
Avoiding confusion and strife.

He'll be your Protector; His angels He'll send,
To watch over you all the day,
Invite Him to be your Companion and Friend
That you may His Spirit display.

True Religion

The scribes were concerned with outward forms,
And desired to be seen of men,
They would pray long prayers to be heard in the streets,
And holiness there would pretend.

They would write many rules for folks to observe,
That they for themselves would not follow,
Pretentious and proud, they impressed the crowd,
But their hearts were selfish and hollow.

They used the poor to gain their wealth,
Robbing widows who placed in them trust.
Though claiming that they were the chosen of God,
He looked upon them with disgust.

God's worst accusations were aimed at the scribes,
For they did not walk in His ways,
For though there were people who needed their help,
They never a finger would raise.

How is it with you, dear Christian today,
Are you seeking for those you can bless,
Or are you contented to pass them on by,
And comfortably go to your rest?

Though it's well to have knowledge of what's in God's Word,
The thing that the Lord will require,
Is that you have served Him by helping the poor,
And seeking their good to acquire.

For if you have cared for the least of these folks,
Christ says you have done it for Him,
By sharing your food and the things that you have,
Your light will not fade and grow dim.

Then humble yourself and be willing to serve,
Jesus left His example for you,
He has promised to guide you and walk right beside you,
If you to His word will be true.

Truth

We dare not stray from truth away; it is the sure foundation,
And what is truth, but God's own Word, ensured for our salvation?
No compromise with heaven's creed, born in the mind of man,
Can think to change the Word of God, once issued by command.

Though vain attempts have oft been made to wrest interpretation,
The ones who seek to know the truth will find an explanation.
An isolated text may seem to say a certain thing,
Yet balanced with all other texts will clarification bring.

The strong desire to know what's right, with qualms all left behind,
Combined with true humility will gratify the mind.
We cannot twist the Word of God to suit our own desire,
To try to change it to this end would be to play with fire.

Though men have tried to chip away at truth God set in place,
His Word is firm as solid rock, not easily erased.
Compliance with God's Holy Word should be our great desire,
The Holy Spirit's presence is the thing which God requires.

For God is God; He changes not for devil or for men,
He wrote His truth upon a stone with finger, not with pen.
Embrace His truth; it's guaranteed to give you joy and peace,
And pleasure in the future life, where wonders never cease.

True Wisdom

The fear of the Lord is the essence of wisdom,
Though you may be otherwise smart.
For it's not only facts in the head that will count,
But love which resides in the heart.

For often a man may have knowledge acquired,
Yet may lack in the things that have weight:
The truths which are written in God's precious book,
On which he should then cogitate.

Though men may be showered with earthly acclaim,
For all of the things that they know,
Yet they may be lacking in value and depth,
While focused on things here below.

Though we live in a worldly environment today,
Our focus should be up above,
In which we find vital direction each day,
When inspired by God's measureless love.

Living for self and the things one may gain,
Whether wealth, reputation, or toys,
Are shallow at best and when given the test,
Will amount to just tinsel and noise.

The only true wisdom comes down from above,
It enriches the soul who partakes,
Of faith that is needed to trust in God's words,
While he much of men's wisdom forsakes.

Though it's good to prepare by becoming aware,
Of the things which are needful to know,
Yet the focus must be on eternity's time,
And not on earth's temporal show.

For the fear of the Lord is the wisdom that counts,
Though you may be otherwise smart,
So store up true wisdom by bending your knees,
And by getting in touch with God's heart.

Unity in Christ

The love of God has been revealed by Calvary's sacred cross,
It opened mercy's floodgates wide, lest we should suffer loss.
Transcending race and differences, uniting all as one,
It overlooks deficiencies as tolerance is begun.

It binds the heart in sympathy, for each man is a brother,
It teaches all to bypass self in favor of another.
In Christ there is no north or south; there is no east or west,
And those who were despised before have bonded with the rest.

In families, love can unify the husband and the wife,
When kindly looks and words are used to banish needless strife.
The children, too, will recognize and copy what they see,
And pass along the kindliness wherever they may be.

For when we love each man as friend, the world will clearly see,
The love of God that's shed abroad by folks like you and me.
The world will want to share our joy as they behold our love,
And pass along God's bonding gift from heaven up above.

Two Kisses

Two kisses were offered the Master,
One from a source He called "Friend,"
Who was given the rare opportunity,
For the Master's will to defend.

When he looked on the Master's talents,
And His power, the people to feed,
He had at that point no intention,
To cause his loved Master to bleed.

He hoped to be high in the kingdom,
That the Master had often portrayed,
He longed for the time when his Master,
Could be found with a king's robe arrayed.

But then when the Master said clearly,
"My kingdom is not of this world,"
He was sad and was most disappointed,
So his mind with a plan unfurled.

He knew that the Master had power,
To deliver Himself if betrayed,
He thought if He forced Him to action,
He'd soon be in king's robes arrayed.

He worked with the envious priesthood,
His devious plan to achieve,
He bargained with them for some silver,
And thus thirty pieces received.

The sign for the wretched betrayal,
Was to plant on his Master a kiss,
No other more subtle portrayal,
Could be as ironic as this.

Though knowing his plan and his purpose,
The Master addressed him as "Friend,"
The words must have stung this disciple,
As the strongest the Master could send.

The kiss from another disciple,
Was totally different from this,
It came from a heart that was grateful,
While bathing His feet with her kiss.

For she was a sinner forgiven,
In her heart she was pure and sincere,
She wanted to lavish affection,
On Him whom her heart held as dear.

For kisses can vary in meaning,
It depends on the motive within,
They can offer a loving affection,
Or uncover a heart full of sin.

You can't fool the Master who loves you,
Pretending to give Him a kiss,
If your life and your actions deny Him,
Salvation will not come like this.

But when you are truly forgiven,
And are grateful for what God has done,
He will know by your words and your actions,
That your new life with Him has begun.

Remember the two kinds of kisses,
Make sure that your kisses are pure,
For then you can rest in God's promise,
That your place in His presence is sure.

Unity or Uniformity

Nobody likes a uniform; it doesn't seem creative,
It never is individualized, nor is it innovative.
The greatest challenge that often comes to Christians here below,
Is through their great diversity, their unity to show.

We all think somewhat differently, yet as we walk with God,
Our thoughts begin to walk in sync upon this earthly sod.
God seems to like variety, for no one is the same,
And yet despite our differences, we're called by Jesus' name.

We often fight to have our way; it takes more strength to blend,
To see an issue as others do and value them as friends.
But unity can be brought about, despite diversity,
Variety of each thinking mind will add some spice, you see.

Can two walk astride in Christian thought unless they are agreed?
It all depends how earnestly upon God's Word they feed.
For those who truly love His Word will find a responsive chord,
In those who have God's Spirit sought as over His Word they've poured.

It's then in joyous harmony, as soul responds to soul,
That men will know the unity and love that makes us whole.
It's then the world will recognize that we have been with Christ,
For then our walk in unity will other folks entice.

Weapons of Our Warfare

Weapons are tools that are often used to coax and to persuade,
To win the heart and conquer minds in the challenge life has made.
The weapons and artillery for Christians of today,
Are those as used by Christ when here, to win the souls who stray.

For Christ was merciful and kind, with truth, His weapon near,
Humility would grace His words, dispelling pain and fear.
The strongest weapon of His life-- self-sacrificing love,
Could melt the heart and satisfy the soul with heaven above.

If weapons worked for Jesus Christ, they'll also work for you,
It's time to put these weapons on, for warfare now is due.
Go forth to conquer in His strength and bring God's children home,
Where they will find a place to rest, no more to stray and roam.

What Devil?

If you ever have doubted a devil exists,
It's easy to see it today,
For evidence mounts in the news every hour,
As evil is viewed bearing sway.

This enemy lurks in the streets of each town,
Wreaking havoc that's hard to deny,
Undetected, he enters each place he can find,
The hope of all good to defy.

He hides in the greed which possesses the men,
Who would steal from the poor to gain wealth,
In the unregenerate heart he also exists,
While absorbed in the pleasing of self.

In the reckless abandon of health, he entraps,
And in revel of sordid affairs,
He captures his victims and makes them his slaves,
Camouflaging with innocent airs.

By the selfish abandon of needs in the world,
Men's desires will be set on their own,
By seeking their pleasure and that without measure,
Their minds in corruption are sown.

With evil surmising and clever devising,
They murder at will on the street,
With modern device, Satan slips in a vice,
So each conscience will fall in defeat.

Because of the evil the devil commands,
Men want to be top of the heap,
Instead of concern for all others around,
Their conscience has fallen asleep.

The devil exists and is hanging around,
Wreaking havoc wherever he can,
Yet God has now offered a way of escape,
That's open to every man.

Though the path will be rocky with bumps on the way,
Requiring a true self-denial,
God has promised a glorious future to those,
Who will walk with the Lord in each trial.

There's a heaven to win and a hell to be shunned,
And it all can be yours for the taking,
Just be sure you are choosing God's heavenly path,
And the devil's agenda, forsaking.

When Christ Became a Snake

Because of their disobedience, God's people were bitten by snakes,
They were dying because of their sins; their lives were all at stake.
Then God instructed Moses, a brazen serpent to make,
He must put it on a pole at once to fix their sad mistake.

By looking at the snake, their lives could then be spared,
But only if they looked could the problem be repaired.
The serpent symbolized Jesus, who would take the sinner's place,
For only by looking to Him could they experience grace.

But why should a horrid snake depict the precious Lamb of God,
Who had no sin at all, while walking this earthly sod?
For wasn't the devil a serpent when talking to mother Eve,
And wasn't the snake a cover so he could then deceive?

"If I be lifted up, I will draw all men to me",
Thus, Christ became our sin in taking our penalty.
It's only as we follow and keep our eyes on Him,
That we can then be healed and let the world grow dim.

When Christ Comes

What are the signs of Christ's coming,
And is it a secret affair?
God's word has told us beforehand,
That trumpets will sound everywhere.

For every man will behold Him,
Whether he's ready or not,
The lightning will flash, an earthquake will shake,
To summon the day man forgot.

For God is not slack with His promise,
For He told us that He would return,
To reward every man as his actions shall be,
To reward him with life or to burn.

The righteous who lived for the Master,
Will rise from their dark, dusty beds,
The righteous folks who are still living,
Will join them as Jesus has said.

The wicked will run from God's presence,
To hide from His powerful light,
They will cry for the rocks and the mountains,
To hide them from glory so bright.

The earth by distress will be shaken,
For the day of God's wrath has arrived,
His presence will execute judgment,
Where evil and selfishness thrived.

He will come as a thief in the night,
To those who neglect to prepare,
But His coming will not be a secret,
To those who await Jesus there.

No second or third chance is given,
To change one's decision that hour,
Today is the day to get ready,
To prepare for the day of His power.

He is eager for all to be ready,
For heaven's a glorious place,
He forever will miss His dear children,
Who have chosen to turn from His grace.

For today is the day of salvation,
Tomorrow may just be too late,
All heaven is there for the taking;
It is you who determines your fate.

When Crisis Comes

Events can surface quickly to try the human soul,
And oft reveal one's character as sad events unfold.
A sudden death in family, a friendship gone awry,
The loss of steady income are sure the heart to try.

The character, once hidden, will surface then and show,
And whether it is admirable, all others soon will know.
Events can be a blessing or turn into a blight,
Depending on the mindset, they're viewed as day or night.

When trials surface quickly, what will be seen in you?
Will you be found in selfishness or with a heart that's true?
The impression that remains, which surfaces to stay,
Depends upon the character that you now form today.

When Heaven Begins

Heaven starts right here on earth when we accept the Lord,
For peace and restful happiness, He will to us afford.
No longer will we feel alone to struggle with our fears,
For God has reassured each one that He is ever near.

Each day can be a waking joy, no matter what life brings,
For in the midst of pain or loss, the heart can rise and sing.
For Christ has paved the way ahead by bearing pain and trial,
That we may overcome with hope in spite of men's denial.

For heaven starts right here on earth; what joy to know it's true,
And if that isn't still enough, God's planned much more for you.
For when the heavens open wide, God's glory will increase,
We'll dwell for all eternity with the blessed Prince of Peace.

When Tempted

When rising from His watery grave upon that special day,
Christ set out for the wilderness to meditate and pray.
To contemplate the mission God had given Him to do,
He dedicated all His will to salvage me and you.

For forty days and forty nights, no food would He then take,
The devil seized upon this chance, God's Spirit then to break.
He tempted Him with hunger, saying, "Turn these stones to bread",
Till Jesus told him only by God's Word must man be fed.

Christ was tempted by His foe to think that God would save,
If He would jump from off a cliff, by twisting words God gave.
When taken to a precipice where kingdoms He could see,
The devil called for homage, saying, " All will come to thee."

If Jesus had responded thus and thought of only self,
Man's chance at his salvation would be hung upon a shelf.
Instead, His only answer was to quote from heaven's Word,
Which silenced Satan of the chance for error to be heard.

In Christ's example lies the plan for man to follow suit,
For only with God's Holy Word can man this foe confute.
Don't parley with the devil, any argument to win,
When Eve agreed to take him on, it led her into sin.

In man's own strength, he cannot hope to conquer or succeed,
For safety only comes by choosing on God's Word to feed.
For heaven will be cheap enough for man at any cost,
And as he lives by heaven's Word, man will sustain no loss.

Where Angels Fear to Tread

Why should you walk in places where the angels fear to tread,
When you can walk with Jesus in the path where He has led?
Some places are forbidden for the enemy is there,
To lure you on his premises and catch you in a snare.

Though you may think it safe enough to go where you're forbidden,
Too late you may discover that the place is evil-ridden.
For life consists of choices that determine destiny,
It's best for follow God's instructions if you would be free.

The dance hall with its music, which is written to entice,
Beclouds a person's judgment like a smooth, hypnotic vice.
The glass of wine so innocent, with bubbles sparkling bright,
Has oft allured the unsuspecting person in the night.

The so-called friend who urges you to do a shady thing,
Should be avoided at all cost with problems it might bring.
Sophisticated cigarettes, which hide their bitter end,
Are often introduced by either family or a friend.

The drug that others rave about and pass along with glee,
Is only the beginning of your pain and misery.
Again, I ask, why should you walk where angels fear to tread,
When you can have the greatest joy—to walk where God has led?

Where Freedom Ends

Perversion isn't freedom where the Bible is concerned,
For some things are forbidden, which by now, we should have learned.
Instead, our culture celebrates the things condemned by God,
Claiming them a natural right while on this earthly sod.

We wonder why the culture spawns such discontent today,
And people protest everything that doesn't go their way.
We give the mother right to slay her unborn child at will,
And then protest the righteous men who would God's word fulfill.

The Bible states that in the end, that evil will grow worse,
When so-called rights that men proclaim are nothing but a curse.
For freedom is a granted thing, which has its limits curbed,
We best stay close within the lines, lest nature we disturb.

Perversion of the gender roles no longer now is hidden,
Defying what the Bible says, in that it is forbidden.
Repeating what God's Word declares is now considered hate,
But in the judgment soon to come, there will be no debate.

For Sodom and Gomorrah were destroyed for such as this,
What makes us think that God, in judgment, will our case dismiss?
For God states that His Spirit will not always strive with man,
Men play with danger when they start to tinker with God's plan.

The rights that God has given men disintegrate to wrongs,
When men ignore God's limits as their sin leads them along.
We need to learn that freedom ends wherever God's Word starts,
And that the change that we must make begins within the heart.

Where Mercy and Justice Kiss

The greatest event on the earth came to be,
When the God of creation left heaven for me.
For my sin, which was heavy, could not be erased,
Till the God of the universe stood in my place.

He would take all my guilt and other men's too,
And receive in my place all the things that were due.
Though the wages of sin should be death heaped on me,
Yet He took all my guilt so that I could go free.

For there on the cross, all my sin was dismissed,
When I found that both mercy and justice had kissed.
For only the life of the sacrificed Christ,
Was able for sin's costly debt to suffice.

The law that condemned me, from which I'm now free,
I joyfully honor and keep willingly,
Not out of debt for the work I should do,
But because of the love He has shown me and you.

And if I should stumble and fall by the way,
I know I can ask for forgiveness today,
For He's made a promise I know He will keep,
His blood is assurance of all I will reap.

For heaven is just the beginning of things,
That makes my heart happy and ready to sing,
The best is the friendship I find in His love,
And knowing He's anxious to see me above.

Women and Church

When it comes to the issue of women and church,
It's not one of rights but of roles,
It's not to the world we should look for the truth,
But in letting the Scriptures unfold.

Though women have suffered abuse in the past,
And have struggled to ascertain rights,
It's well to remember that God has a plan
To put all confusion to flight.

Though women have rights, they also have roles,
Which God has designed them to play,
The pattern was set in the garden of old,
And continues on down to this day.

For Adam was called to be head of the race,
While Eve was to stand by his side,
Her role was to be His companion and friend,
While Adam would care for his bride.

Since Adam was placed as the head of the race,
After sin, he was called to account,
Though Eve was the first in transgression, we note,
On Adam, the weight seemed to mount.

All down through the years, men were priests in the home,
Their role was to lead and protect,
The woman would care for the family and home,
While each showed the other respect.

It was men whom God chose to be rulers and kings,
The disciples He chose were all men,
It wasn't the culture that caused Him to choose,
For women, as well, were His friends.

In Eve's sad transgression, she doubted God's word,
And expected her role to be higher,
But she started a trend which was not soon to end,
By cherishing selfish desire.

A woman is called to fulfill many roles,
Which in some ways are higher than man's,
For she constantly shapes what the future may hold,
By the children she guides with her hands.

You don't have to be at the top of the heap,
Just use all your talents today.
If you are determined to give all to God,
He's certain to show you the way.

Be satisfied, ladies, with what God designed,
There are blessings in what you can do,
Do your best for the Lord and be found in accord,
And His praises will fall upon you.

You'll find comfort and peace in doing His will,
And when, in His judgment, you rest,
You'll find at the end of your journey on earth,
God's decisions were all for the best.

Wrestling with God

Have you ever wrestled with your God, till all is on the stretch,
And in the process realized that you're a sinful wretch?
If you're honest in your thoughts, with this revealed, you'll see,
Some things that hide within the heart are not what they should be.

You know the things of which I speak: the pettiness and pride,
Impatience, temper, jealousy--the things we tend to hide.
The less than noble thoughts that tend to lead the heart astray,
The wasted time, the angry mood when things don't go your way.

The overreaching greediness that must a bargain make,
The irritation often felt when making a mistake.
This wrestling match, though challenging, is in the Father's plan,
For all these things are common in the heart of every man.

The hopeless feelings that arise when looking close within,
Result from deviation from God's plan, which leads to sin.
Man's only hope is in the life of Jesus, Lamb of God,
Who conquered all temptation when He walked this earthly sod.

The wrestling time, though painful now, will cause the soul to see,
That Jesus Christ, man's only hope, has come to set him free.
For when the soul of man surrenders to God's mighty power,
God's seed of holy righteousness in man begins to flower.

For in those searching, trying hours, God's Spirit lingers near,
To turn the helpless soul to Him who takes away all fear.
Then one by one, the evils in the heart begin to die,
And man will come off conqueror as eternity draws nigh.

Your Identity

What is your true identity, and what is it measured by?
Is it found in what men think of you? Can you on them rely?
Are you known by your education, or perhaps by the people you know,
Or is it by the way you talk or the talent which you may show?

To be of value to God and to man while you are here on earth,
Is to recognize your truest self by valuing things of worth.
When you accept God's plan for you and trust His healing power,
You'll find your true identity in that very day and hour.

The relationships you have on earth can distort your picture of you,
Causing your true identity to be lost in what you do.
But if your identity rests with God, then all will fall in place,
And the person you were meant to be will show by joy on your face.

Your Temple Today

How strong is the temple you're building today?
Is it built to endure in life's storm?
Will its walls tumble down when the strong winds assail,
When tragedy sounds an alarm?

Has your faith been established on truth in God's Word,
Or on the inventions of man?
Have you placed all your trust in the blessed Lamb of God,
Who can cause your temple to stand?

Is your hope in the promise of heaven above,
Understanding God's Word cannot fail?
Will you cling to the knowledge that He will be there,
When nothing around you prevails?

Please understand that you're fragile and weak,
Unless you're depending on Him.
You need to establish your faith in His Word,
And not on caprice or a whim.

He has promised He never will leave or forsake,
He offers you strength to endure.
You can trust Him to do what He's promised to do,
For you know that His promise is sure.

You must give Him your heart for it's already His,
For He purchased it there on the cross,
Then your temple will stand in the palm of His hand,
Protecting and saving from loss.

REFLECTIONS ON LIFE

A Bird's Eye View

A bird crashed on my windowpane and hit it with her beak,
She longed to find a place to nest, a cozy place to seek.
She did not seem to understand the nature of the glass,
And that it would not let her through, allowing her to pass.

She hit the glass repeatedly as if to get her way,
Determinedly, she kept right on and flew there every day.
I finally closed the window blinds, her efforts to deter,
Not only for her good but mine, to keep things as they were.

As this went on from day to day, I questioned her persistence,
To put herself in jeopardy without the least resistance.
It made me think how often we, as children of the King,
Have put ourselves in danger's way and to our follies cling.

We often push persistently against God's mighty arm,
When He has placed His barriers to keep us out of harm.
We blindly seek for happiness in dark, forbidden places,
Until, confused, we find ourselves bereft of heaven's graces.

O foolish men, how slow we are to see the Master's plan,
Until we fall and find that we may need a helping hand.
Far better would we fare if we would read God's Word today,
Respecting all the barriers He's placed along our way.

A Christian Marriage

How sweet is a true, Christian wedding,
When hearts are united in love,
When angels are happy to join them,
Looking down from heaven above.

When music that's sacred and holy
Enhances the gathering there,
When the union is blessed by God's presence,
And invoked by a meaningful prayer.

How sweet is a true, Christian wedding,
When hearts can revere the same God,
When folks whom they love will support them,
While walking on life's shaky sod.

When promises vowed are regarded
As sacred as any they know,
And simplicity marks their beginning,
Instead of pretentious show.

How sweet is a true, Christian wedding,
A blessing to all gathered there,
When the pair has united their interests,
And are willing their talents to share.

No greater example is given
To represent joy seen above,
Than that of a true, Christian wedding,
When hearts are united in love.

A Fine Kettle of Fish

The baby wants his bottle, and he doesn't mind complaining.
The child demands a special toy and will resist restraining.
The parents want vacation time with cherished peace and quiet.
With everyone dissatisfied, it's sure to start a riot.

It seems no one can wait to have the thing which he desires.
Impatience tends to rule, and no one's putting out the fires.
Why is it we as humans tend to struggle with this trait?
It seems no one is willing to restrain his need to wait.

When Eve was in the garden not so very long ago,
Contentment filled her heart until impatience seemed to grow.
She could not wait to taste the lovely apple from the tree,
Which God had warned her not to eat that she might trouble flee.

Impatience is a form of doubt that leads us not to trust
That God will have our best in mind because He's good and just.
For when we run ahead of God, not satisfied to wait,
God cannot work His will for us while we His plans debate.

"Be still and know that I am God"; His word to us is clear,
And if we are attentive, we will turn our heads and hear.
But when we rush ahead of God, He's forced to use plan B,
Which might involve a rocky road, which we won't wish to see.

Impatience is a leprosy that grows with steady use,
And for this great malignity, there is no proven use.
It's always best to wait on God; let chips fall where they may,
So we may be prepared to meet Him on that special day.

A Mother's Reflection

Since mothering days are over, I don't have to be the Sarg,
It's time for me to just be a friend, and no longer be in charge.
It's time for me to now relax and enjoy the children I grew,
And watch them raise their children now like I have had to do.

I can dote on my grandkids, spoil them a bit, and brag on what they do,
I can reminisce on past events, recalling the things we've been through.
I can thank the Lord for all He has done in giving these children to me,
And pray that we all may gather above to enjoy eternity.

A Solemn Choice

There is a time for everything
That happens under the sun:
A time to be born, a time to die,
It comes to everyone.

One of the most important times
In which one finds a voice,
Is when you give your heart away,
In that, you have a choice.

The tricky part is in choosing well,
For outward demeanor can blind,
Yet there is a ready solution in which
A true love you can find.

You can make the Lord your partner today
And take His counsel to heart,
By choosing one who draws you to Christ,
Not one who draws you apart.

Don't give your heart to another soul
Who doesn't believe as you do.
Hold fast to the truth you believe in,
And always to God be true.

For it's hard to walk together as one,
If not in the same direction,
In time, you may find you have drifted apart,
And have lost your first affection.

Determine to put God first and best,
No matter how feelings may go.,
In the end, you'll be much happier, too,
And the sure results will show.

For feelings cannot be relied on,
And can often the heart deceive,
But putting your trust in the Word of God
Is something you can believe.

Pray more than you've ever prayed before,
If having a smidgen of doubt,
And ask for wisdom from God above,
The deception of Satan to rout.

For marriage can either be heaven or hell,
Depending on how you will choose.
Your choice will reflect on the life you live
As to whether you win or lose.

A Tribute to Dad

Who but father knows the joy of gazing on the face,
Of the tiny, precious creature he has added to the race?
Especially if it is a boy with whom he can relate,
His satisfaction knows no end, not open for debate.

Although he'll think he has it all by fathering a boy,
He has no clue how much a girl can also bring him joy.
For girls can savor many things-- like fishing, sports, and bikes,
They also have been known to take to camping and to hikes.

No matter which one nature can supply him at the time,
His heart will swell with gratitude, and pride will meet its clime.
For nature has a special way of binding to the heart,
The helpless creature God decides to grant him from the start.

God bless each father as he learns to guide his treasures rare,
To nurture and to love them well, to handle them with care.
That one day when he's growing old, his days will be much blessed,
By knowing he has done his job by giving them his best.

A Woman's Lot

There are dishes to do and laundry to fold and beds to make in between,
There are floors to mop and kids to correct and even potties to clean.
On top of it all, there are meals to fix, and groceries to get besides,
Sometimes, it seems, she could just run off and cover her face and hide.

A woman's lot, while humble, it seems, can keep her on the run,
Though keeping busy from morning till night, her work is just begun.
Even though multi-tasking all day, ten hours will hardly suffice,
To do what seems demanded of her, and keep the house looking nice.

And when at night, she falls into bed, exhausted and craving rest,
The baby awakes, demanding to feed at the ever-available breast.
Though tired and spent, her mind is content to do the best she can do,
To minister to her family's needs though minutes for self are few.

For she is a Christian mother who's proud of the role that she can play,
To be a model of industry, while doing her work each day.
The long range goal that lights her fire is to lead her family by love,
To walk in the path that Jesus walked and be ready to meet Him above.

A Word in Time

Rules of etiquette always abound
Whenever it's people you meet,
Whether you find yourself eating with friends
Or run into them on the street.

Conversing with friends is a delicate thing,
Involving some give and some take,
If you're tending to hog the floor all the time,
You'll find it has been a mistake.

For everyone has an opinion to share,
And it's never considered polite,
To use up the time which others should have,
For it shows that you're lacking insight.

As the old saying goes, at a social time,
If you're hoping to have any clout,
It's best to be quiet and be thought a fool
Than to blab and remove any doubt.

You may think that it's clever to speak all the time
If no one corrects what you say,
But if this is your habit, you'll find in due time,
That people will go on their way.

For people are eager to share what they think.
When talking, it's hard to learn more,
And if you will listen to hear what they say,
You won't be considered a bore.

It's best not to risk the loss of a friend
If your tongue is not under control,
Remember, good listeners are always in style
If the truth of conversing is told.

So button your lip and tune up your ear,
Give others a chance to be heard,
Your presence to all will be a delight,
And people will hang on your word.

A Word to the Wise Woman

As you arrive at dating age, let wisdom be your guide,
And be aware of choosing friends in whom you will confide.
Don't be persuaded by attention men may have toward you,
Don't be a feather in their cap, but to yourself be true.

Though hormones race and beg permission to be satisfied,
Be guided by your self-respect; let passion be denied.
And hold yourself in high esteem; don't give yourself away,
Though you are charmed by so-called love, he may just want to play.

For marriage is a life-long pact that calls for self-respect,
The goal for happy marriage is to put such play in check.
Take time to get acquainted with your long-range goals in mind,
Determine that the one you choose will be a special find.

And if he truly loves you well, then he will gladly wait,
To satisfy that special longing past the marriage gate.
For he may lose respect for you if you should once give in,
In addition, God has warned that fornication is a sin.

God's ways are best, and you will find your happiness depends,
On taking counsel in your plans when choosing special friends.
Then let God's Spirit help you find the one He's planned for you,
And wait for marriage to enjoy a love that's warm and true.

Action and Reaction

Actors and reactors dwell upon the earth below,
Actors show their colors while reactors are but slow.
When an issue comes to surface, bringing challenge to each man,
Actors often speak their minds; reactors fear to stand.

Actors have opinions, while reactors rarely do,
From folks who seem decided, they seem to take their cue.
Sometimes, it is a noble thing to take a stand that's bold,
At other times, it's best to wait and put your words on hold.

Whether you're an actor, or you tend to just react,
It's best to hold your tongue a while until you know the facts.
The challenge comes in being wise in knowing what to do,
Whether you should take a stand, or keep your thoughts with you.

When urged by strong conviction that you have to take a stand,
You must weigh the situation and obey your heart's command.
If you waffle at the moment, and your chance to speak is lost,
You may find that in the future, you may have to pay the cost.

If you have read the Word of God and have its wisdom heeded,
You'll know just when your silence or words will then be needed.
Your words can be a blessing, and your silence can be too,
The trick is to discern the need to know which one is due.

Another Anniversary

Another anniversary, upon a mission found,
Reminds us of the special day in which our hearts were bound.
Though years between have come and gone, we still remember yet,
The treasures of that magic day, which we will not forget.

The throbbing pulse within the heart, the long expectancy,
Of joyful days awaiting us still fill the memory.
The friends around, well-wishing us, the food and special cake,
Still flood our hearts with precious gems our hearts cannot forsake.

Recapturing that precious day reminds us of the time,
When we did catch the essence of the Father's heart sublime.
In gratitude, we thank Him for His gift of human love,
A taste of what awaits for us when we arrive above.

Autumn's Magic

The golden time of autumn casts its spell upon the trees,
The leaves now red commence to dance and play upon the breeze.
They swirl about in circles wide and pile up in the street,
While those who would engage their rakes are destined to defeat.

The blend of orange, red, and gold, a subtle touch of brown,
Announce the coming ravages of winter's waiting frown.
The summer's kiss of warmth and sun has all but fled and gone,
As autumn flings her colors bright and moves the seasons on.

The lazy, watermelon days have disappeared from sight,
While shorter days of longer sleep extend the hours of night.
As changing colors set ablaze the hills in riot fair,
Anticipation fills the heart with expectation rare.

For soon, the cooler, autumn days will bring the winter rain,
While coats are drawn from closets dark, one's comfort to sustain.
The fire at night will bring delight, and knitting will appear,
As cycles of the seasons flow to grace another year.

The magic of this golden time will linger in the mind,
Long after harsher days have come, the season to define.
Though winter comes and ushers in the snow and freezing rain,
The joy of fall's nostalgic hours in memory will remain.

By the Sea

A seagull flew as the fog drifted in,
And blotted the landscape from view,
The rocks in the ocean like sentinels stood
Eclipsed by the moist, foggy dew.

The monotonous waves blew foam on the shore,
Leaving bubbles like glass on the sand.
No sounds could be heard but the waves and a bird,
As the fog settled in on the land.

A pungent aroma escaped from the sea,
Reminiscent of visits before.
The salt on my lips conjured memories of old,
From other such trips to the shore.

The breeze whispered lightly of fish and of crabs,
While sending my hair in my face,
Blending memories of old with the new, fresh and bold,
Which cannot be quickly erased.

Carpe Diem

We live our lives in a flurry, it seems, planning for things ahead,
We always anticipate future events until the time we're dead.
We seldom stop to think about the moments we spend today,
Before its minutes and hours expire and thus are swept away.

We often regret the miles we go, instead of enjoying the trip,
We tend to gulp our lemonade down instead of savoring sips.
It's hard to smell the roses while we're rushing through the field,
Expecting on another day, to smell the scent they yield.

Before we know, we've gotten old, with nothing to show for the tasting,
We start to feel that precious time is what we have been wasting.
Though it's good to plan for tomorrows, don't forget about today,
For it just may be you'll feel a loss when time is taken away.

Choices

The mind is a fertile, open field where many seeds are cast,
Yet only seeds with nourishment will grow their roots and last.
The things on which the mind may feed are chosen by each one,
And will produce a harvest crop when once they have begun.

For that on which the mind will feed is sure to bear some fruit,
Because it dwells on certain things and keeps them in pursuit.
The choices enter everyday to form the goals and plans,
The character will then be seen by that for which one stands.

If given proper nourishment, the mind will bloom and grow,
By choosing to instill the things that healthy minds should know.
The opposite is true as well; if garbage is the food,
The mind will shrivel up and shrink with sad ineptitude.

For God has given each a mind in which to give Him glory,
By feeding it upon His Word and telling men His story.
The world consists of good and bad; each choice in time will tell,
And God will then be glorified if one has chosen well.

Divorce

Divorce is such an ugly word, I shudder to define it,
For when a marriage breaks apart, it's hard to realign it.
The children suffer most of all, no matter what the cause,
That fact alone should give the parents reason for a pause.

It may just be a little hurt that one should soon forget,
That grows into a larger one and causes much regret.
Desire to have one's selfish way, despite the consequence,
Can cause a barrier to rise as attitudes grow tense.

Until at last a wall is raised which neither one will climb,
To reestablish joy that once was thought to be sublime.
Communication then breaks down; a coldness settles in,
Until it seems too late to try another round to win.

Divorce was never in God's plan; He said, "I hate divorce,"
For when a marriage tears apart, there is no smooth recourse.
The children languish in the wake, suspecting they're the cause,
That mom and dad can't get along as happiness withdraws.

A scar remains forever in the ones who are affected,
And that includes the relatives with whom they are connected.
Be careful whom you marry, friend; be sure to take your time
To choose a partner God approves and keep your love sublime.

Down the Road

What can you do when you're down in the mouth,
And your mood is more cloudy than bright?
The day can be warm and inviting outside,
But inside your heart, nothing's right.

You can kick all the rocks down the road as you go;
You can stew on the thoughts that are sad,
You can sulk, you can brood, but it won't help your mood,
If you do, things might really seem bad.

It's better to just go outside in the sun,
And summon a breath of fresh air.
As you walk, you will feel new contentment and peace,
As you wander in nature out there.

For troubles will come; they come to us all,
It's not an unusual thing,
What matters is that you let troubles pass by,
And resolve to go on as you sing.

For this trouble will pass, and life will go on,
Most things are resolved with some time.
Don't carry a grudge, but give it a nudge,
it's not worth a reason or rhyme.

Look up in the sky, the day still is bright,
You'll find a new joy if you do,
Remember this tip if some trials should come--
A song will your spirit renew.

Dreams

Dreams can be good as far as they go,
But sometimes they aren't enough.
For often they carry a bit of hot air,
And sprinkles of white, fairy fluff.

You need to give serious thought to your dream,
And whether you're fit for the task.
It could be another might fit fairly well,
Providing much more than you'd ask.

Some things can look promising seen from afar,
But clouds may be blocking your view,
And then when the hot air and fluff all dissolve,
Will your dream be the best for you?

Remember that God has a plan for each life,
Which He makes for each person with care,
But if you don't ask for His guidance today,
It's certain you won't end up there.

Because He has made you, He knows you well,
You're the apple within His eye.
He knows where you best will be fitted to work,
And your happiness, He will supply.

Suppose that His plan is the dream that you chose,
You'll still need His leading today,
For then He will certainly help you succeed,
And will guide all your steps on the way.

He knows where your gifts and your talents reside,
For He settled each one in its place,
It's up to you now to acknowledge somehow,
That His plans you will seek to embrace.

And if you consent to His leading today,
You will find in the end that it's true,
You'll be living the dream that was always God's plan--
The one that He's planning for you.

Harmony

May I not squelch another's song, his voice to thus deny,
For each man has a song to sing, his soul to satisfy.
May I encourage him to sing the song that makes him glad,
The one that brings him happiness and covers what is sad.

And when I wish to sing again, may I respect his song,
That we may blend in harmony as we two walk along.
If solos tend to rule the day, no unity exists,
It's only as we blend our notes that harmony persists.

Then raise your voice in joyful song, and I will raise it higher,
That we may spread the happiness that tells of our desire.
And then, when voices rise no more and all is mute and plain,
The echo from our harmony will linger and remain.

Endangered Species

We fret about the spotted owl, lest it become extinct,
Including other creatures that may teeter on the brink.
Though rightfully we share concern, a larger problem looms,
It comes with more importance and must our thoughts consume.

For what about our babies? Are they not endangered too?
With helpless human life at stake, the more concern is due.
It seems absurd that for a bird, our sympathies arise,
Yet no one seems to notice if another infant dies.

Has life become so meaningless because it's not our own,
That we give little notice though atrocities are known?
What will it take to come awake to stop this tragic loss,
When selfish and imagined rights have brought this hefty cost?

Though we decry the holocaust, repulsed by such a thing,
Our silence speaks of our consent when suffering it brings.
We ought to shake our heads in shame, for we have lost our way,
When countless such atrocities continue every day.

It's time to rise in unity and waken from our sleep,
Repenting from the grievous sins which now upon us creep.
Return to treasured values that this country once embraced,
And stop this shameful tragedy by which we are disgraced.

First Love

It's said there's no love like the very first love,
When passion awakens you,
And time can't erase that loving embrace,
Which seems all at once to be true.

You'll always remember that magical time
When everything seemed to be right,
When nothing could steal the happiness found,
And all was sweetness and light.

As time went along, and feelings had changed,
You moved on to somebody new.
You hoped that because of that very first love,
You'd find love again that was true.

For often a first love has wings that can fly,
Yet seldom returns to the earth.
It lacks the stability life will require,
Ignoring the things of great worth.

The best love to own is a practical one,
Which will pay all the bills that come due,
The love you can live with brings joys that will last,
Which by far is the best of the two.

Though first love is magic and floats through the air,
You'll find when it's all said and done.
The love that will last when compared to the past
Is always the practical one.

"Honey"

When we were young, we heard our mother call our father, "Honey",
So we began to do the same, not thinking it was funny.
It never seemed as strange to us, for we were children then,
Because we always called him that, the name caught on with friends.

It always seemed most comfortable that "Honey" was his name,
Whether he worked around the house or played a baseball game.
For even the team on which he played each Sunday in the park,
Managed to take the name in stride when "Honey, you're up!" was barked.

It posed a problem on a night when my folks attended a party,
For a guest kept hearing "Honey's" name, when everyone was hearty.
It was "Honey" this, and "Honey" that, by which she was amused.
"Whose honey is he, anyway?" she asked, while quite confused.

When I was engaged to my future spouse, I took him to meet my folks,
When I told him what we called my dad, it seemed to him a joke.
At first, he felt uncomfortable in calling my father, "Honey",
But after a while, he was used to it, and then it wasn't funny.

So, what's in a name? Why, everything! Or maybe nothing at all,
It all depends upon the man on whom the name may fall.
In the case of the loving father I knew, a honey of a man,
It's everything, I tell you now, and on this fact I stand.

If Gossip Should Strike

Live so that if you are gossiped about,
Folks will find that it's hard to believe,
Convinced that the things that are whispered about,
Are generally meant to deceive.

If you're honest in all that you say and you do,
Giving people no reason to doubt,
Your actions and words, long established before,
Will soon put the gossip to rout.

Though you cannot control every devious soul,
You can live far above their remarks.
You can order your life so it's empty of strife,
If you're steadfast in all you embark.

Keep your character white, and the gossip will pass,
And time will throw doubt upon those,
Who find it a pleasure to gossip in measure,
While jealous of those they oppose.

A character steadfast is hard to deny,
Despite what another may say,
Just keep your head up, ignoring what's said,
And soon it will just fade away.

In time, truth will conquer, and all will be well,
And patience will win in the end.
And who knows? The one who had gossiped at first,
May turn out to be a good friend.

In Dedication

At last, our precious baby girl has finally come to stay,
She charmed us from the very first with her endearing way.
Her ready grin, her searching eyes demanded our attention,
They indicated eagerness and ready comprehension.

She filled up any empty spot that needed to be filled,
She brought new life into our hearts and left us warm and thrilled.
It wasn't long until she had us wrapped around her fingers,
And when we had to be away, her presence with us lingered.

She is a joy to bathe and dress from headband to her toes,
The joy that she has given us, why, only heaven knows.
We dedicate her to the Lord, for she is first His child,
We long to do the best for her, this creature, sweet and mild.

Then Father, take our lives today that she may always see,
Your love revealed in both of us in what you'd have us be.
And when this life is over, may heaven open wide,
So we may walk your golden streets with her, right by our side.

Intimacy

Intimacy is meant to be the fruit upon the tree,
Reserved for couples taking vows to last eternally.
It is the icing on the cake to bind two hearts in love,
The fruit of sweet companionship, endorsed by God above.

For God has placed a sacred hedge around the marriage vow,
In which no other must intrude, where none is there allowed.
It wasn't meant for entertainment for the folks unwed,
But rather was reserved for couples having marriage beds.

Though stolen fruit appears as sweet, it later then will sour,
And leave a sad regret and shame that conquered in the hour.
Keep fresh the fruit for one you love; don't spoil it by misuse,
But keep it special to enjoy with one you finally choose.

It then will bind your hearts as one, no matter what the weather,
By smoothing problems that arise and keeping you together.
What God has joined together by vows, let no man tear apart,
Guard sacredly the sanctity of intimacy in the heart.

Language

The challenge of language is often derived
From its flexible nature and use,
It quite often suffers from license we grant
To indulge in its ready abuse.

The meaning of words that we read can be changed
By a comma, which has been misplaced,
Confusing the reader by twisting the thought,
Producing an error, embraced.

With language so supple and up for debate,
Who is there to judge what is right?
By giving a speaker the freedom to change it,
Pure language may drift out of sight.

Despite this prediction of what may occur,
Perhaps rigid rules shouldn't be,
For when open to change, new words may arrange
For some bright creativity.

When people are coining a word for their use,
It often is pregnant with meaning,
They often take license to use what relates
To other words, gathered by gleaning.

Though language is apt to take wings and to fly
And often its muscles to flex,
It's wise to stick to the basics as well,
Or it's hard to say what may come next.

Masquerade

We wear a mask to hide the hurt which we have felt and known,
We place a smile upon our face, lest bitterness be shown.
We cover up our darkest hours by shielding them from light,
To keep them all from surfacing and bursting into sight.

Yet in this dark and secret place, they fester and they grow,
They rob us of relationships, which once we used to know.
They steal from us the joy and peace which once was known before,
By dwelling on the pain and hurt which knocked upon our door.

Our fragile soul cannot embrace the freedom we should hold,
While baggage clutters up the space and leaves our spirit cold.
When will we learn to let it go? ---Forgive and just forget,
That we may then embrace the joy our souls still long for yet.

One of a Kind

Because there is no one exactly like you,
You truly are one of a kind.
And since this is true, in reference to you,
God must have had you on His mind.

Because you are special, it's foolish to seek,
To become someone different from you.
Develop the talents with which you are blessed,
And give God the credit that's due.

Since things which are rare and complex in design,
Have value because they're unique,
Be happy inside with the person you are,
Do not new identity seek.

Be thankful God made you the way that He did,
He wants to make use of your gifts,
And when you devote them to bless other folks,
Your efforts will give them a lift.

For God has a special design for your life,
In which all your talents are used.
You must ask Him to guide and walk by your side,
Be not by distractions confused.

Enjoy who you are, and others will, too,
Yet be not conceited and proud,
And let not the world with its charm and allure,
Your practical sense becloud.

Since you're one of a kind, you must keep this in mind,
If you want to be all you can be,
Don't spend your time moaning for what you don't have,
But use what you have joyfully.

Since all of God's children are one of a kind,
We must value each soul as of worth,
For if we would value each one that we meet,
There just might be peace on the earth.

Mother's Model

Since mother's gone, I now can see
How she, in life, affected me.
For one, she never raised her voice,
Thinking it a tactless choice.

Taking pride in family scenes,
She kept surroundings neat and clean.
Practical in dress and taste,
She never let things go to waste.

Prudent in the things she bought,
She always chose with careful thought.
Generous when arose a need,
She would share a thoughtful deed.

She was social and was kind,
Yet unafraid to speak her mind.
Loving justice, she was fair,
Unassuming, showing care.

Classic in the things she wore,
Modest dress became her more.
Unaffected by position,
She displayed no proud ambition.

Honest as the day is long,
She could not endure a wrong.
Settled in the truth she knew,
She would share when such was due.

Self respectful, she would rise,
Favored in the public eyes.
Sought by friends for her advice,
Wisdom was her trade device.

Since she's gone, I understand,
In all of this she had a plan.
Through all these things, I now can see,
She modeled what she hoped I'd be.

Parenting

Parenting is a challenging task,
For no two kids are alike,
And just when you're sure that a problem is solved,
New problems are ready to strike.

For kids don't arrive with a manual book,
And no parenting books will agree,
On how to resolve the teenage years,
And the onset of puberty.

Most children are born with a willful streak,
That must often be curbed and restrained,
It's how you will handle that delicate need,
That will prove if they're rightfully trained.

Some children are easily guided and led,
While others can need stronger measures,
Yet each must be taught to choose right from wrong,
In order to gain life's pleasures.

It's a balancing act with love sprinkled in,
With patience required and restraint.
It isn't a job for the indolent soul,
Or for those who by nature are faint.

It's only by keeping in touch with God's Word,
That a parent can hope to succeed,
For it's there in its pages of wisdom and love,
That an answer is found for each need.

No parent is perfect, with fixes that match,
Every need that may seem to arise,
We all make mistakes by doing the thing,
At the time which seems right in our eyes.

Yet the Lord is forgiving and fills in the spots,
That are empty where we seem to fail.
He asks us to do the best that we can,
So that future success can prevail.

Our children are precious, a gift from the Lord,
From whom we can learn every day.
It's only as we try to emulate God,
That success comes to brighten our way.

We need to refer to His words on our knees,
While seeking to follow His plan,
Then as a reward, when heaven comes down,
We will walk with our kids, hand in hand.

Political Correctness

When you silence the settled convictions of men,
You've basically robbed them of choice,
And if men are derided for honest beliefs,
You essentially silence their voice.

If you say what you think in the world of today,
And it's not what the crowd wants to hear,
You may face disapproval by shaming or threat,
Though you hold what is spoken as dear.

For politics deems what is proper to say,
In this world of divided opinions,
And what should be said is chosen today,
By those in heady dominions.

Persecution today can take varied forms,
Though they aren't as harsh as the rack,
Yet the mind isn't freed to embrace honest creed,
When having to watch for one's back.

For scanty indulgence of other men's thoughts,
Is a dangerous concept to take,
For it limits the way conversation may go,
When speech is considered mistake.

Our culture is reaching a hazardous place,
When we limit the words men may speak,
For the freedoms we cherish are starting to perish,
When choosing this narrow technique.

For even the Bible, whereon in the past,
This notable country was formed,
Is now disregarded by some in this place,
While other things take on the norm.

When good is called evil and evil, called good,
And men who are right are called wrong,
Society weakens, and good men are blamed,
While evil still marches along.

It's time to return to the freedoms and rights,
Which have caused this country to grow.
Away with the silence and bring back the speech,
Respect that which once we did know.

Bring honesty back and a healthy desire,
To return to our once Christian roots,
For only the freedom we once did embrace,
Can error and evil refute.

Power of the Tongue

Have you ever been known to embarrass yourself,
By blurting out untimely words?
And when they have barely escaped from your lips,
You wished that no one would have heard?

The tongue can move quickly before one has time,
To think of the things he should say,
To sort out the message that should have been said,
And the one he should banish away.

Far better is he who can temper his tongue,
Than he that can capture a city,
For often when tongues are unloosed without thought,
It's a scene to encourage some pity.

A thoughtless remark can discourage and wound,
And often, no cure can be found,
To heal all the damage that might have occurred,
When untimely words did abound.

It's better to hold all the thoughts in one's head,
And decide what is fitting to say,
Than to blurt out the first thing that pops in the mind,
Which shouldn't see light of the day.

Though the tongue may be small, it is mighty in power,
It can hurt or can bless those we know.
The tongue must be bridled and duly controlled,
For love and compassion to show.

Though having intentions to say the right thing,
We often will blunder ahead,
And it isn't uncommon to struggle with this,
Until our last words have been said.

The only solution is putting a guard,
On our lips while inviting a prayer,
To the God who can help us with all of our needs,
By knowing that He will be there.

His Spirit will take control of our tongue,
And give us the words we should say,
And if we should stumble, He'll raise us again,
To walk in His own perfect way.

It's then that our words can be beautiful things,
That will grace all the folks that we know,
By scattering blessings that God has prepared,
For all of His children below.

"Rights" vs. Wrong

Though folks may be granted the "right" to be wrong,
Some things are still wrong in God's eyes,
For the evils of men who insist on their way
Will never take God by surprise.

The premise of "rights" accorded to men,
Must be passed through the sieve of God's Word,
When neglected, men clamor for things God condemns,
Granting practices that are absurd.

For God has forbidden some things for our good,
To eliminate wrongs that abound,
When they are not heeded, then evil is seeded,
And sin in our country is found.

When politics campaign in favor of sin,
And by protest of people are swayed,
God keeps a true record of what has occurred,
And wrong in the balance is weighed.

For we're told in the end that the children of men,
With evil will wax worse and worse,
Until they have spread its influence abroad,
To incur disapproval and curse.

When right is called wrong, and wrong is called right,
And God's Word is left in the dust,
We've only ourselves left to blame for results,
When neglecting God's counsel to trust.

Settle for More

Don't settle for less when you can do more,
Determine to rise a bit higher.
Who knows the great heights that you may achieve,
By having a fervent desire?

The first aspiration with which you begin,
May not be the best you can do,
Much more might be had to make your heart glad,
And bring satisfaction to you.

Sometimes when a failure occurs in your life,
It can be an incentive for change.
To throw out the old and bring in the new,
To regroup and then rearrange.

"Always improve" is the motto to take,
For who knows the good you can do?
Throw doubt to the wind when once you begin,
Press forward until you are through.

For nothing is gained if you choose to remain,
Accepting what's now status quo.
If you forge on ahead to achieve a new goal,
You'll discover how far you can go.

The sky is the limit, so set your goals high,
And if obstacles get in your way,
If God is your Guide, He will be by your side,
For He always will have the last say.

Sisters

Sisters know each other well and never seem apart,
Though miles may separate the two, they're always close in heart.
The atmosphere in which they grew, the people they once knew,
Have given them a reference point which nothing else could do.

Their sense of humor is the same, because of circumstance,
They seem to know what will amuse the other in advance.
They may not look the same, and yet, there is a golden tie,
Which binds them close together, and which no one can deny.

At times they may just disagree, but always in the end,
They know each other will be found to be a cherished friend.
Though different interests in their lives may find them each unique,
They know that for the other one, the best of things they seek.

Through thick or thin, through good or bad, whatever may befall,
They know in crisis there is one on whom they first can call.
Because they are the best of friends, no others can compare,
With sisters bound by blood and love to other folks elsewhere.

Story Time

Each person has a story, which he or she could tell,
Of failures and successes and tragedies as well.
For no one's life is perfect, and problems come to each,
The end result depends upon the goal one strives to reach.

You cannot judge expressions or tell from whence they come,
For often folks will wear a mask to keep from looking glum.
Each one has known some heartaches, if he has lived for long,
And some will try to hide their grief by whistling a song.

It's only when you get to know a person really well,
That you may hear a story true, which he may choose to tell.
For as we grow, we learn to be like actors on the stage,
Who, often with reality, on screen will not engage.

It's only in the quiet hours and only in the dark,
That people with reality will finally embark.
It's best to never judge them; conclusions may be wrong,
It's better far to lift them up and help them find their song.

The Better View

Some people see the stars at night while others view the dark,
Some folks succeed in reaching goals while others miss the mark.
It all depends on attitude and how one looks at life,
You either find the good in it or find it filled with strife.

The glass can be half empty, or perhaps half full instead,
You choose the way you look at things: with hope or nagging dread.
The end result can satisfy or bring a great regret,
For you will find that in this life, your choice is what you get.

If such is true, then in my view, a positive view is best,
You might as well choose the brighter side, the negative to contest.
It's better to keep a smile at hand and forget the dreary frown,
Your smile will keep your spirits up while frowns will let you down.

If you are always positive, you'll find that in the end,
You'll help some folks along the way and make of each, a friend.
You'll make your mark, though it be small, and while you're having fun,
You'll find the joy that life can bring and one day hear, "Well done."

The Cost of Love

What is the history of Valentine's Day?
Is it more than flowers and hearts?
When studied, you'll find that it's more than that,
So how did this holiday start?

When the Emperor Claudius ruled over Rome,
The man Valentine was a priest,
The Emperor commanded that during that time,
All marriages had to cease.

He felt that the men who were single were apt,
To make better soldiers for him,
Than those who were married, who might be involved,
Because of their wives and their kin.

Because the culture was sinful and loose,
The priest would encourage instead,
For Christians to marry, which caused him in time,
To finally lose his head.

He secretly married the couples at church,
Until he was finally caught,
He then was imprisoned and tortured in jail,
For doing the things that he ought.

One of the judges who took on his case,
Had a daughter who then was blind,
When Valentine prayed and the girl was healed,
The judge was to Christians inclined.

The priest Valentine would write his last note,
To the maiden who once had been blind,
The note was the start of this sweet holiday,
And the words which one often will find.

The content it held, we're not privy to know,
Yet we know how the letter was signed,
The words are familiar, you've heard them before,
It stated, "From your Valentine."

So enjoy all the sentiments, candy, and flowers,
That Valentine's Day will bring,
But remember the priest who stood for the right,
And did not to comfort cling.

For love has its price and some suffering, too,
There's a lesson that's hidden herein,
One must always take care to stand for the right,
Even to losing one's skin.

The Death of Modesty

What happened to modesty, seen in the past,
In which, self-respect was expected to last?
The girlish allurement of ruffles and lace,
By sexy attire is now often replaced.

The sweetness attending the charming, first blush,
Is often regarded as old-fashioned mush.
We now are the moderns, outspoken and bold,
Who care not for counsel, regarding it old.

Why has sweet modesty flown far away?
The hemlines grow shorter, it seems, everyday.
The necklines, by contrast, are dropping as well,
And where it may finish is not hard to tell.

The charming allurement of modesty's face
Has now all but vanished by sexual embrace.
Nothing is left to imagine or guess,
It now can be flaunted by style's modern dress.

The soft, fitting garment that gracefully flows,
Is gone for the moment, as everyone knows.
The dresses are tighter, each layer is known,
The hems move up higher as more skin is shown.

And when one is seated, the dress is so short,
It often can lead to unwholesome retort.
It's not hard to notice the spiral leads down,
And ladylike essence is starting to drown.

Where is the mind that will limit the dress,
To one that is modest and thus can be blessed?
Each one a choice and it's left up to you,
To make up your mind and decide what to do.

Don't be a temptation to men who may wane,
Who need extra courage, their eyes to restrain.
But set an example to all whom you meet,
A ploy of the enemy now to defeat.

The Listening Ear

Trials come in this old world with challenges galore,
And just when one is rectified, it seems that there are more.
A listening ear is needed then in which to pour one's troubles,
To help a person sort them out and let them burst like bubbles.

What does it take to be a friend one tells his troubles to,
Who listens with a caring ear until the person's through?
It isn't one who's fidgeting while you relate your story,
So he can tell his own sad tale and revel in its glory.

It isn't one who plans to share the problems he may hear,
Or one who will respond with his own problems or his fears.
It's one who listens carefully while dedicating self,
And for the moment puts his personal cares upon the shelf.

It's one who waits and listens well, connecting with the heart,
Who empathizes with concerns in which he has no part.
He then responds with wisdom, having gleaned from God above,
Encouraging with helpful words, the joy of Jesus' love.

The listening ear can either be a blessing or a curse,
If selfishness gets in the way, the problem will be worse.
Then listen up, forgetting self, and be a friend in need,
By doing so, you will be blessed by planting heaven's seed.

The Missing Piece

When you find a piece is missing in the puzzle you have done,
It seems to spoil the picture, though the piece is only one.
The picture then is incomplete and will not be the same,
It lacks a vital part and tends to lose its final aim.

Our lives are like a puzzle till we find the missing piece,
Which will satisfy that empty spot and cause our stress to cease.
We struggle for the answers to our questions in this life,
Yet find ourselves still empty, in confusion and in strife.

We look for men's acceptance, thinking that will bring us joy,
Or save to find the money that will buy a treasured toy.
We often search through many books to find the answers there,
Yet find ourselves still troubled by a constant, nagging care.

The missing piece is Jesus Christ, the Savior of the soul,
You'll find He is the only One who makes the sinner whole.
That empty spot He longs to fill, your questioning to cease,
For He Himself has placed it there to fill with joy and peace.

The Press

"If it bleeds, it leads" just seems to be the motto of the press,
And for the need of sordid facts, one doesn't have to guess.
Outrageous, public criminals rely on press to gloat,
On every ugly detail of their heinous acts of note.

The sad replay of vicious scenes on which offenders feed,
Will foster other wretched acts by watering the seed.
When interviewed, no sad remorse is shown, but rather pride,
That they have now accomplished what a better mind would hide.

Atrocities, thus glorified, have often been repeated,
By less than stable, upright minds, where virtue is defeated.
No poor excuse of openness or freedom of the press,
Can thus excuse the sharing of these details in excess.

The press has been responsible for loss of good discretion,
In which the public's right to know amounts to sad transgression.
The need to be sensational to shock the eye or ear,
Has fostered some revolting scenes that folks disdain to hear.

By beholding, we are changed by things on which we choose to dwell,
We need to feed the mind on that which keeps our thinking well.
Lest we become what we behold, it's time to turn about,
To dwell on things that edify as sordid things we rout.

It's time to just report the news and leave the gore behind,
For better things will benefit and bless the thinking mind.
Till then, no exaltation of a horror need be spread,
But rather, let the positive and helpful now be said.

The Royal Wedding

A wonderful royal wedding was planned,
The prince and his lady would wed.
The town was alive with excitement and glee,
Discussing the news that had spread.

And even the people from countries afar
Took note of the happenings there.
They counted the days till the eager, young prince
Would marry his lady fair.

Unique preparations were made for them,
From flowers and food to her dress.
The place for the wedding was chosen with care,
With details arranged to impress.

With all the excitement and media buzz
Of this royal event that would be,
It caused me to think of another event
Being planned for you and for me.

For one day not far in the future of time,
A wedding of note will take place.
The groom is the King who is soon to wed
The bride He has salvaged by grace.

This marriage will be more impressive by far
Than all of those made in the past,
Because of the promise in Jesus' own words,
This marriage in heaven will last.

The Single Parent

No matter what the reason is, she finds herself alone,
The single parent, left for good with children on her own.
She's devastated by the blow, emotions all awry,
She's lonely now and has no one on whom she can rely.

The children are bewildered too; they cannot understand,
The fact that daddy now is gone, omitted from the plan.
She gazes at the stack of bills; how will she ever manage?
For having just one income now will be a disadvantage.

She wonders if she'll have to move but knows not where to go,
And if she'll marry once again, it's hard for her to know.
The kids seem more dependent now, much more so than before,
They're moody and they're anxious, wondering what will be in store.

She'll have to be both parents now with no time left for her,
She'll have to face life all alone, with no one to concur.
She has no time to weep and cry or sympathize with self,
For there is just too much to do; such things are on the shelf.

She'll have to make the best of it till answers fall in place,
Till then, she'll have to carry on and fill the empty space.
The single parent bears a load that none can know while married,
And few will ever realize the weight that she has carried.

It's left to us to look around to see if there's a need,
To help a single parent out by thoughtful Christian deeds.
It just may be by doing so, that we can offer hope,
And salvage one who's almost at the end of such a rope.

The Snowstorm of 2019

The challenging snowfall of twenty nineteen,
Was the largest that we could remember.
We little suspected the weather would change,
Since it had been warm since September.

In late February, around one o'clock,
The temperature started to drop.
A heavy snow quickly embellished the yard,
As other activity stopped.

The trees bowed their branches, all laden with snow,
Which fell through the day and the night,
Until it had piled up for two feet or more,
And blanketed all in our sight.

This measure of snow, though considered as small,
By folks who reside in the East,
Was to people like us, unaccustomed to snow,
A problem which grew and increased.

Large trees which had fallen then blocked up our drive,
We were stuck and unable to go,
And even if somehow, the driveway were clear,
We couldn't escape for the snow.

All was well for a day till the power went out,
And the house then began to lose heat.
So we revved up the generator, kept for such things,
While hoping to save food to eat.

Though grateful to harness a new source of power,
A fact that was readily seen,
Was that sooner or later, we'd need to have fuel,
In the form of some more gasoline.

Not able to leave, we summoned someone,
Who walked in some much needed fuel.
By this time, it seemed, with the turn of events,
Mother Nature enjoyed turning cruel.

Since we needed some heat, we thought of our stove,
But not planning to use it this year,
We had covered the chimney with screen early on,
To keep out the birds living near.

The question arose, if we started a fire,
Would it draft through the screen and the snow?
If the fire didn't draft, would the house fill with smoke,
Not having a good place to go?

We pondered a while as to what we should do,
Yet needing the heat, went ahead.
Though it worked for two days, yet one night, we awoke,
When smelling the fumes from our bed.

We both had solutions for what we might do,
In the end, my husband prevailed.
Needy times call for desperate measures, they say,
When emergency comes to assail.

My husband decided to climb on the roof,
To remove the debatable screen.
So in two feet of snow at two in the night,
Though I tried, I could not intervene.

With heart in my throat and prayer on my lips,
I watched him ascend up the ladder,
By shining a flashlight high on the roof,
I hoped to assist in the matter.

I breathlessly watched as he gingerly walked,
Step by step on the roof through the snow.
Though reluctant to watch, I was riveted there,
For he still had a long ways to go.

He finally descended the ladder that night,
With the screen now successfully moved.
He returned safe and sound, yet no cause can be found,
For having this method approved.

With the problem now solved, we aired out the house,
And gratefully headed to bed.
But then in the morning, we found we must deal,
With some problems that still lay ahead.

Since constantly needing more fuel for the house,
With no way to get down our road,
We decided to summon someone with a plow
To clear a path to our abode.

The contractor came with a price on demand,
Which by then we were happy to pay,
It was worth it to us to have use of our road,
So that we could then make our own way.

Once the road had been plowed and the trees were removed,
We decided to go into town.
With the gas cans on board to fill up while there,
Another new problem was found.

A large tree had fallen atop of the roof,
Of the pump house and straddled the drive,
We had to drive under the tree to depart,
While hoping that we would survive.

Though the tree stayed in place, we found it unsafe,
To travel with it overhead.
We called in a friend who removed it for us,
Relieving our minds from this dread.

We shoveled a path from the house to the shed,
Loading wood for the stove every day,
For weeks we would bathe from the water we boiled,
Wishing power would come back some day.

It was during this time of challenge and snow,
That our 4-wheel Toyota would die.
It had to be towed to the dealer in town,
With no parts in ready supply.

One thing I've discovered while living through this,
Is a pioneer woman, I'm not,
But when push comes to shove, you work hand and glove,
And give to it all you have got.

Because we were waiting for power to come,
And hoped it would soon come to stay,
We decided, though sometimes the snow has its place,
We'd be happy when it went away.

We were thankful that God had provided for us,
By keeping us safe through the storm.
Perhaps He allowed this to teach us to trust,
In His almighty, capable arms.

We also were grateful for folks whom we called,
Who were willing to do a good deed.
For friends are the ones who are ready to help,
When a person is found in great need.

After seventeen days, the power came on,
The snowstorm had finally passed.
Life went back to normal, whatever that is,
Our nightmare was over, at last!

Things of Worth

Life on earth will not be viewed by things that you have owned,
But rather by the helpfulness which you have gladly shown.
Nor will your value be esteemed by beauty of your face,
But rather by the needy souls you blessed by your embrace.

For value isn't measured by the shallow thoughts of man,
But rather passes muster when on heaven's word it stands.
The selfish heart of man is focused largely on himself,
No room for God is figured in as being of great wealth.

The greatest joy and happiness is found in serving others,
Who by creation's thoughtful plan are sisters and are brothers.
No buildings, clothes, or vehicles, no art of beauty rare,
Though they bring satisfaction can with brotherhood compare.

For life must always pass the test by what is in God's book,
Its values are what really count; its truth, don't overlook.
Your worth in life is measured by the things which God holds dear,
Be sure you choose the things of worth by keeping heaven near.

Together Forever

I noticed the name of the shop as I passed,
"Forever Together" it said.
With marriages constantly going awry,
It caused me to doubt what I read.

I'm sure good intentions are probably meant,
By those who might take on the vow,
Yet time seems to somehow unravel and thwart,
Each promise that's spoken somehow.

Are roses and moonlight the culprits, you think,
Or is it the wine in the glass?
Or is the engagement too short to resolve,
The problems that might come to pass?

I'm sure the excitement and glamour that come,
With the thought of a wedding of bliss,
Can go to folks' heads before they are wed,
Especially after a kiss.

It's enough to erase all the questions that come,
As to whether the two are well suited,
To wrestle with challenges life can present,
When problems become convoluted.

It's best to slow down if one is inclined,
To rush into such situations.
It's better to wait, considering well,
The future's intense obligations.

The best way to know of the way one should go,
Is to seek God's desire in your plans.
He will lend you His voice in making your choice,
And will make of your life what is grand.

Together forever is not just a dream,
But is always what God had in mind.
If you will surrender to Him your desires,
Much peace and contentment you'll find.

Tolerance

Since men live in circles, which no one else knows,
The hidden is covered; we see that which shows.
What frames each existence, we rarely can see,
Perspective is never what it ought to be.

Because we don't walk in another man's shoes,
It's easy to make the assumptions we choose.
With judgments shortsighted, which typically are,
We rarely see closely, but see things afar.

Since this is the case, it behooves us to see,
Our judgment is not what it's cracked up to be.
It's better to lay down the gavel and rest,
And leave them to heaven and those who know best.

Vantage Point

Mothers have a vantage point which children cannot share,
Maturity never is revealed till one is finally there.
The wisdom that will come with age, a child can't comprehend,
For only time can peel away what seemed a mystery then.

When young, the will is very strong and cannot understand,
That mother needs to often cross the things that youth may plan.
Distraction is the better way instead of confrontation,
But mother's word must still be law, despite the agitation.

It's only when a child is grown, he may appreciate,
The guidance that was given him or times he had to wait.
For mother always knows what's best, and all will come in view,
When children of their own are raised, and wisdom then is due.

What Every Girl Wants

Every girl wants to be pretty,
You'll find that it's just in the genes.
She admires the sweet ballerina,
And the elegant, graceful queens.

In her quest, she'll buy cosmetics,
And ornaments by the ton,
New clothes, new shoes, new hairdo,
And the search has just begun.

She'll copy the latest styles,
To be sure she's in the groove,
She'll busy herself with activities,
To show she's on the move.

What the world considers as beauty,
She insists on imitating.
She seems to miss the obvious,
Which others may find frustrating.

Though it's fine to be blessed with beauty,
What the world first needs is love--
The kind and helpful spirit,
That flows from heaven above.

For beauty is but transient,
It comes, then goes with age,
Which no cosmetic can salvage,
Or other effort assuage.

For the quality folks remember,
Is the kindliness of deeds--
The small considerations,
On which the spirit feeds.

The character is the essence,
Of what's involved in beauty-
The thoughtfulness to others,
The attentiveness to duty.

Though the world may relish beauty,
Assigning it highest claims,
Remember that value is written
On a well-respected name.

For character is that which lasts,
Long after beauty is gone,
And it's only a Christ-like character,
That can be depended upon.

What Men Desire

A man wants a woman who's sure of herself
In a humble, but positive way,
Not one who attracts by her beckoning laugh
To draw his attention away.

Though he may be flattered by women who flirt
And throw themselves in his face,
The woman who's modest, just being herself,
Has charm that is hard to replace.

He looks for a woman who's modestly dressed,
Respecting the charms she holds,
Not one who will show every asset she has,
Or one who is overly bold.

A man wants a woman for whom he must strive,
Not one who's an easy catch,
A woman who shares in his values and thoughts,
Whom he will consider his match.

He's drawn by one who can laugh at herself,
Which proves that she's not too proud,
Yet pleased at her strength to put stops in place,
In front of things never allowed.

He looks for a woman, attractive and clean,
Who owns some ambition and goals,
Not one who depends on another and clings,
While keeping a desperate hold.

A man wants a woman to think for herself,
Who can share in a deep conversation,
Yet not one who holds her opinion so high
That she's eager for argumentation.

A man wants a woman who's loyal and true,
A model for children to come,
Ambitious to keep the house tidy and clean,
And while doing so, not to be glum.

He looks for a woman who's upbeat and bright,
Not one with a negative tone,
A woman to share in his work and his play,
Who keeps herself for him alone.

He looks for a woman with whom he can share
His private and intimate thought,
With whom he has confidence she won't reveal
The personal things he has brought.

A man wants a woman, who later in years,
Can still share his friendship and love,
Who, when his is down or discouraged by life,
Will point his attention above.

A man needs a woman in whom he can share
A love that will last till life's through,
Looking forward together, no matter the weather,
To share life in heaven anew.

When Calls the Heart

When calls the heart, do not be swayed by feelings or by sight,
For hearts can be most fickle and cannot discern the right.
Don't give your heart too easily for what appears as gold,
Can sometimes turn to tinsel when the truth is finally told.

The heart lacks wisdom, always stirred by thoughts of sweet romance,
It needs a sieve to strain the dross that comes by circumstance.
It needs a guide to lead one to a suitable conclusion,
To seek avoidance from events that end in disillusion.

The only guide dependable is that of God above,
The One whose very character is that of endless love.
If called upon, His Spirit will be there to guide you through,
To guide you to the very one most suitable for you.

No other way is guaranteed to bring a happy end,
To find for you a loving heart, designed to be your friend.
Do not depend upon your heart, for it may fickle be,
Depend upon the God above to guide your destiny.

White Lies and Others

Honesty is always the right way.
When you're guilty, it's best to confess.
Rather than using deception,
If honest, you're sure to be blessed.

For it's hard to remember when lying,
The lie that you told once before.
If you're honest, it won't be a problem,
Ad problems won't lie at your door.

A white lie amounts to a black one,
For each has deception to hide.
What is judged at first to be harmless,
May conceal some darkness inside.

Though it seems naïve to be honest,
In the end, you'll find that it's true,
That no one appreciates lying
When business involves me and you.

The intent to deceive is a lie.
It amounts to the very same thing,
For when you're not open and honest,
Your intent has a dubious ring.

Don't parley with lying and stealing,
When involved, some damage is done.
A heaven exists for the winning,
And a hell remains to be shunned.

For the greatest lack of the world today
Is the lack of men who are true,
But the righteous can always be trusted,
In what they're attempting to do.

So remember, when tempted to lie,
To cut a corner, or steal,
It's better to be fair and honest,
The spirit of right to reveal.

Wisdom

Wisdom announces her peace in the morn
Before the world is awake.
She whispers a blessing to all who will hear
And would of her riches partake.

She cries in the midst of the world that's astir
In the heat of the busy day,
To bring to the mind what is honest and fair
In the din of work and of play.

She is there to recall her gems of delight
To the soul who leaves open the door.
She begs to come in, lending guidance within,
When men keep her counsel in store.

Impartial to all, she is happy to call
On each who will walk in her ways,
To all who will treasure her gift to mankind
And use it to brighten their days.

Then in the storm, when the soul is alarmed,
Her presence will quiet the heart.
She will bring needed peace and whisper release
As problems and stress depart.

Then go to her house and drink of her wine,
Enjoying the fruit that will last,
She'll lead you and guide you and walk beside you,
If you will her essence now grasp.

Woman's High Role

The role of a woman is sacred and high,
For she sets a new trend for the nation.
She raises the children that make up the sum
Of the hopeful and next generation.

For what other role can be greater than this—
To mold and to guide future thought,
To make the world better than what was before
And model the good that is taught?

It's fine to develop the talents you have
To find your fulfillment in life,
To make you feel useful while helping the world
To live above challenge and strife.

But what really matters are those who are placed
Within your protection and care,
The ones whose development truly depends
On the training and love that you share.

This unequaled challenge to women at large
Is not often valued or sought,
And yet much depends on the time they devote
To this wonderful gift God has wrought.

Let finance not rule the exceptional school
On which the world's future depends,
For home is the place that a woman can grace
By the nurture and care she expends.

Let mothers be proud for the privilege allowed
In watering plants of God's making,
Be greatly assured that results will endure
In this solemn and grand undertaking.

And if mothers have faithfully given their all,
Be confident heaven won't rest,
Till all of the children they've carefully trained
Are safely at home in God's nest.

Words

Words cause war, words make peace, words wield vital power.
They change the course of history within a single hour.
Words can charm and warm the heart, caressing it with care,
Words can also stab and wound, destroying what was there.

Words can cause a face to glow or paint it with a frown,
They make the spirit rise and soar or cause it to fall down.
For words are regulated by what lives within the heart,
They must be disciplined by love, which only God imparts.

The natural heart defaults to self without God's intervention,
It takes a touch of holiness to steer words from dissention.
For words can be a benefit, or they can be a curse,
They either calm hostilities or they can be perverse.

The filter on the tongue must be a prayer upon the lips,
For God to intervene and keep the tongue from making slips.
Then words can be the blessing that they all were meant to be,
To cause the folks around each man, the face of God to see.

CHRISTMAS

A Christmas Treasure

Tray was a boy in his early teens,
And Christmas was on the way.
His home was in the wilderness,
A little from town away.

He worked at the local grocery store
Till five o'clock each night.
He walked in the snow, three miles or so,
With his father's lantern light.

He was saving the money that he had earned
With Christmas on his mind.
Early on, he'd seen a special watch,
The best that he could find.

He gazed through the window every night,
When passing the local store,
Each time he looked, his heart would leap,
Desiring it the more.

The day before Christmas, he planned to buy
The special, treasured piece.
Each time he thought about the watch,
His eagerness increased.

On arriving home, his dad announced
That he needed help from his son,
To take some food to a family in need
Who was known by everyone.

Tray's dad had heard of the family's straits,
Their need for clothes and food.
He asked his son to take some bread
To the father and his brood.

Shrugging his shoulders reluctantly,
Tray left with the package small.
When he arrived, he met with a sight
Which memory would long recall.

The baby, wrapped in a blanket thin,
Lay whimpering from the cold.
The moldy bread the children ate
Looked more than a little old.

The two year old, in diapers still,
Was barefoot as she played.
With the mother on her sickbed now,
The father was sad and grave.

Tray groaned inside, and his stomach churned
To see the family's plight,
He left the package and quickly turned
And stumbled home in the night.

As he dressed for bed, with prayers all said,
it seemed that he couldn't sleep.
He thought about the family he'd seen
As the hours began to creep.

He tossed and turned on his bed that night,
Hearing babies cry from the cold,
Seeing children playing, poorly dressed,
Eating bread with blackened mold.

When morning came, he quickly dressed
And to the grocery went.
After work, instead of the treasured watch,
His money was otherwise spent.

He bought some shoes for the two year old,
For the baby, a blanket new,
A toy he chose for the little boy,
For the mother, some medicine, too.

A bag of groceries, piled up high,
On the borrowed sleigh he drove,
And a candy cane for each of them
With a stack of wood for the stove.

When Tray arrived to share his gifts,
A smile encompassed each face.
The children excitedly danced about,
Giving each one an embrace.

His task now done, Tray turned to go,
And his heart began to sing,
For Tray had found that sharing joy
Was more than a watch could bring.

Christmas Again

The season of Christmas has come once again,
But all is not merry and bright,
Although decorations appear in the stores,
Yet happiness seems out of sight.

For tragedies near and afar seemed to grow,
With hurricanes, floods, and with fire,
And thousands, bereft of their loved ones and home,
Have lost all their Christmas desire.

The politics rage on the news every night,
Accusations fly this way and that,
Until it is hard to know who to believe,
And rumors are hard to combat.

The racial contentions continue to grow,
With hatred and murders that spread.
The nation's disgrace has brought shame to its face,
While rendering its citizens dead.

The spirit of Christmas with goodwill toward men,
Just seems to have vanished and fled,
The scenes of unrest and the rumors of war,
Have encouraged a feeling of dread.

How did it happen, and why are we here,
In this circle of fear and dismay?
The answer lies closer than what you may think,
You don't have to look far away.

The Bible reveals that the Spirit of God,
Will not always strive with mankind.
It tells us that evil will wax worse and worse,
While compassion will lag far behind.

The idea of Christmas brought tidings of peace,
But men have strayed far from its goal,
For selfishness strips men of kindness and love,
Leaving men who are thoughtless and cold.

It's time to reclaim all the things that were lost,
The peace and the joy that we knew.
Don't look to another to clean up the mess,
For the answer involves me and you.

We must go to the manger in Bethlehem town,
And find Him in swaddling clothes there,
Recalling how He left heaven for us,
To salvage us from our despair.

Then see Him oppressed in the garden at night,
Bowing low with our burden of sin,
Sweating great drops of blood as He wrestled for us,
That we might the victory win.

Then follow Him up onto Calvary's hill,
As He's nailed to an old rugged cross,
See Him writhing in pain and in agony there,
So our souls could be ransomed from loss.

For the peace and the spirit of Christmas, we find,
Can be salvaged in no other way,
Than to bow at the feet of the Savior and weep,
And ask His forgiveness today.

We then can recover the blessings we've lost,
The peace and the hope that we knew,
It's His joy to restore when we choose to obey,
For His love yearns for me and for you.

God's New Year

How fast the year has faded now; the new has come to stay,
As you look back upon the year, what would you have to say?
Would you rejoice in what you've done, in progress you have made?
Or do you have some sad regrets, some debts that should be paid?

If all has not gone well this year, it's time to turn around,
A new year now has come about, where progress can be found.
Don't dwell upon the sordid past, mistakes that have been done,
Look forward to a better day when victories shall be won.

Get down upon your knees and pray; God's power there awaits,
If you will ask, He'll give directions, making pathways straight.
Get into heaven's precious Word; God's message is for you,
He only asks that you will choose to be sincere and true.

Dedicate your life to Him; He'll open up the way,
For you to watch your acts and words to guard what you may say.
He'll cleanse your heart of things that spoil, replacing them with joy,
Destroying all that would confuse and otherwise annoy.

The New Year will bring benefits, unknown to you before,
And as you get into God's Word, you'll progress all the more.
Don't pass this opportunity to grow your wings and fly,
And God will bless the efforts made as on Him you rely.

Irony in the Manger

We often see depicted when it comes to Christmas time,
A lean-to wooden roof of sorts to arch the Child sublime.
But facts reveal another shelter, used by men of old,
In which to house their animals to keep them from the cold.

It seems a natural cave was used, a place already there,
Where heaven's Child with animals, a humble room would share.
And there, among the animals, created by Himself,
The Majesty of heaven lay, bereft of fame and wealth.

The irony that He would leave the courts of heaven's splendor,
Became salvation's priceless proof of His complete surrender.
The thought alone of contemplating what He left behind,
Is quite enough to make one gasp, while boggling the mind.

While that, it seems, was bad enough, it only was the start,
For He would end up on a cross, with crushed and broken heart.
The many wounds along the way just made Him more decisive,
To carry out His sacred plan, when men became derisive.

The taunts, the jeers, the mockery, and then, at last, the cross,
Would seem the devil's victory, while viewed by men as loss.
What men considered loss that day, ironically, would save,
For by His death upon the cross, a road to God was paved.

The infant in the manger, an enigma to be sure,
Though disadvantaged in His life, has heaven made secure.
For by His life and by His death, His glory we can see,
And by these two, great, priceless gifts, we grasp eternity.

Just Beyond the Manger

Beyond the infant manger, heaven's hosts with joy await,
Bending low to hear responses, far from heaven's gate.
Humankind has been delivered from the weight of sin,
In a contract made in heaven, mankind's soul to win.

Will provisions go unnoticed by distracted man,
Who has settled into lust, ignoring God's command?
Will he choose the holy treasure, recognizing worth,
Or disregard its value while he spends his time on earth?

Just beyond the manger, man's decisions must be made,
To value heaven's offering in the price that has been paid.
For each will give an answer by the way that he will live,
And in the many choices of his willingness to give.

Don't disappoint the infant now, the conquering I AM,
Who left His home to salvage you, becoming heaven's Lamb.
For just beyond the manger, there's a place prepared for you,
Where you can join the heavenly hosts with all the righteous, too.

Message in the Manger

It is said to have been in the fall of the year,
When the baby Christ Jesus was birthed,
For shepherds were out in the fields herding sheep,
When the angels arrived on the earth.

The presence of snow and of green, holly wreaths,
Was a far thing from anyone's mind,
When a cave that was housing some animals served,
As the only place Joseph could find.

And only the humbly clad shepherds that night,
Would hear heaven's glorious song,
While solemnly watching their flocks in the fields,
And moving their sheep along.

When the heaven-sent light had burst into sight,
They were shocked and were sorely afraid,
Then the beams disappeared and faded away
As a lingering impression was made.

For the shepherds alone were blessed on that night,
To hear heaven's message of hope,
To enlighten each man, as a part of God's plan,
Enveloping all in its scope.

The world of today, having wandered away,
From the message proclaimed in the night,
Has neglected the truths of the gospel of love,
Which was heralded by angels so bright.

The message unheeded has now evil seeded,
And left men in hopeless despair.
It's time to return to the values once learned,
In the truths that its message will share.

Until that is done and each heart has been won,
By the Savior who came long ago,
We're destined to own all the seeds we have sown,
And a destitute future to know.

Though the message is bleak, there is still time to seek,
For the Savior who came in the manger,
Don't keep Him at bay and at arm's length away,
For He wants to be more than a stranger.

But open your heart to the things that He taught,
You will find they are housed in God's Word.
If you take time to read and its message to heed,
You will find it's the best ever heard.

Revelation of Christmas

What can one say of Christmas time,
That's never been said before,
Of angels bright with shining light,
And peace forevermore?

Of the maiden mild with infant child,
Placed carefully in her womb,
By heaven's command, for the love of man,
Whose destiny was a tomb?

It's an old, old, story, replete with glory,
Which through the ages will live,
For its lessons are truth and mercy and love,
Which God was willing to give.

It has nothing to do with Santa Claus,
Created to steal God's thunder,
Who tries to distract from the miracle,
Of heaven's glorious wonder.

The tinsel, the baubles, the mistletoe,
The extravagant light display,
Are worlds apart from heaven's design,
When Jesus arrived that day.

To a world in darkness, bereft of hope,
This infant would carry the light,
That would fill the world with glowing beams,
Piercing the pagan night.

For years He quietly lived at home,
An example of industry,
Helping His earthly father at work,
While doing it cheerfully.

And when it was time on the heavenly clock,
He took on His role as Messiah,
On the cross He would die at the hands of men,
Where He couldn't rise any higher.

For the cross was His crown, providing the path,
To His exaltation and glory,
He suffered with nails, which His limbs would impale,
As an end to His earthly story.

He was born to die, yet He came for love,
That the sinful men on the earth,
Could catch a glimpse of what they could be
By what heaven would give for their worth.

What wondrous love! Let it soften your heart,
As you see what a price was paid,
That sinful man could be salvaged from death,
By the covenant heaven has made.

Then rejoice this day! Let naught take away
The beauty and pathos therein,
That man can be swept up to heaven with God
Bereft of sorrow and sin.

Signpost in Bethlehem

Come with me now to Bethlehem town,
To the place where Jesus was born,
Not to a stable that's often displayed,
But into a cave forlorn.

It was here that animals stayed for the night,
Kept from the weather and prey,
And thus it was here in this lonely place,
The Gift of heaven lay.

This rough beginning was only the start
Of what was yet to be,
For the place of His birth was only a sign
Of His sacrifice for me.

In the life He would live, He would constantly give,
Desiring for love in return,
Yet what He received would make His heart grieve,
As folks His love did spurn.

Though crowded by curious multitudes,
Christ, nevertheless, was alone,
For none understood His mission in that
He came for sins to atone.

For even His closest disciples would fail,
When He needed them the most,
And of the people He'd come to save
Were none of whom to boast.

And yet He came, while knowing the cost,
The shame, the rejection, the hurt,
Tortured by those He had come to save,
When passion and pride did assert.

When He chose to leave heaven, my sins to bear,
In humility even to die,
For the likes of sinners as you and me,
I can't help but wondering why.

If ever in doubt of His love for me,
I only need look to the cross,
In which heaven sacrificed all in one Gift,
So I would not need to be lost.

It started in Bethlehem ages ago,
In sacrifice, suffering, and woe,
And ended in victory by way of the cross,
By pointing the way I must go.

Special Delivery

He didn't come by accident; He didn't come by chance,
He came by special providence, announced far in advance.
For long before He came to earth, the prophets would foretell,
Of God's great plan to ransom man while here on earth to dwell.

No other child arrived as He, through miracle conception,
No other was announced by great, angelic song reception.
It was a cause for gossip, for rejection, and for scorn,
But He would come at any cost upon that fateful morn.

For prophecy declared that when the promised Savior came,
An angel would announce His birth and even give His name.
He came, the second Adam, by His death to reconcile,
The lost, yet cherished children that the devil had beguiled.

Each thing to Him that happened in His birth, in life, in death,
Was told of Him for many years before He took a breath.
The world was wrapped in dire straits, in darkness, and in pain,
He came to lighten up the dark and make the pathway plain.

His message was of kindliness, of justice, and of love,
He straightened out the crooked ways and pointed eyes above.
The Lord of all creation was the hope of every man,
He lived by God's commandments as He followed heaven's plan.

Unique by any measure, He would empty out His soul,
And offer up His life for all to make the sinner whole.
No one was ever like this One, nor will there ever be,
Another like the Son of God: a special delivery.

The Night before Doomsday

'Twas the night before doomsday and all through the earth,
The angels were seeking for men of true worth.
The signs of God's coming appeared in the land
To give a reality check to each man.

The people were busy with usual cares,
Not giving a thought that the angels were there.
For some were absorbed with their phones or with sports,
While others were seeking amusements of sorts.

The preachers had given their final appeal,
In hopes that their words on each conscience would steal.
But no one was listening; the noise was too loud,
The only thing heard was the reveling crowd.

With violence and force, the disasters began,
To fall on the people and spread through the land.
The feasting and drinking at last were arrested,
To which angry protests then strongly attested.

The earth reeled in anguish and violently shook,
As rocks tumbled down from each cranny and nook.
The mountains and hills were all moved out of place,
As expressions of terror were seen on each face.

In the midst of the panic, a dark cloud was seen,
Heading to earth, unsurpassed and pristine.
And as it came closer, much brighter it grew,
Lending excitement and hope to a few.

A small group was trembling with unrestrained joy,
Which nothing about them could kill or destroy.
For there in the cloud, now glowing and bright,
Were millions of angels with garments of light.

Right there in the center of heavenly things,
Sat Jesus, the Lamb, and the King of all kings.
His countenance was shining; His garments were white,
And the small group responded with sudden delight.

No words can express all the joy and the wonder,
As they gazed up in awe, in the midst of the thunder.
No more would they wander as pilgrims to roam,
For soon they would head to their heavenly home.

Some graves broke apart and the righteous arose,
With new life responding from head to their toes.
They joined with the group who was standing in awe,
At the heavenly host, which they gratefully saw.

Then rising together, they entered the cloud,
While leaving behind them, the wicked and proud.
And I heard them exclaim as they rose out of sight,
"Praise God, Hallelujah! We head home tonight!

The Origin of Christmas

Though I don't wish to rain on your party today,
There is something I think you should know.
It might come as a shock or as a surprise,
Or it might be an unwelcome blow.

But Christmas is not what you think it to be,
A season of fun in the snow.
For it seldom is blessed by a manger of straw,
Though witnessed by earthlings below.

How should people relate to this holiday time,
When it conjures up varied emotions?
For Christ was not born on Christmas Day,
Despite all our fervent devotions.

According to history, it seems that the Child
Was born in the season of fall,
So how did Christmas originate?
Is it worth celebrating at all?

Most of the customs attached to this time
Have evolved from a pagan source.
Combining these things with the birth of Christ,
Can be traced to Satan, of course.

The pagans observed the Christmas date,
As the birth of their pagan gods,
But the early church never honored the date,
To observe it would have been odd.

But later, in Rome, many pagan beliefs
Were adopted into the church,
To appeal to the Christians, it linked them to Christ,
This fact can be found if you search.

There are plenteous symbols derived from this source,
Which taint of licentiousness,
Such as holly and ivy and mistletoe,
Which God could not possibly bless.

One symbol of old St. Nickolas, too,
Can be traced to a rebel of God,
Who came on the scene after Noah's flood,
His name being that of Nimrod.

The name of Santa, if now rearranged,
Spells Satan himself, if you please.
And most other Christmas symbols as well,
Can be traced to the devil with ease.

The Romans, the Druids, the Celtics as well,
And also Egyptians of old,
Embraced these beliefs and, after a while,
The church took them into its fold.

And even the mass in Christmas derived,
In the ancient Egyptian mass,
In which the wafer was round like the sun,
From the worship of sun in the past.

The Roman church adopted these rites,
And eventually made them her own.
It mixed in the sacred with the profane,
Thus knocking Christ off of His throne.

The notion of Yule logs and that of a tree
Are included with others as well.
They are easily traced to heathen beliefs,
Of which their history will tell.

The person who calls himself Christian today,
May blindly ignore pagan ways,
While becoming a spiritual prostitute,
Regarding the Christmas days.

For Christmas today is currently seen,
As a pleasant event to the eyes,
While the practice of rites and evils of sin,
Are cloaked in a holy disguise.

Since the customs of Christmas are firmly engraved,
Accepted by people today,
Will Christians respond to its dubious past?
Should Christmas be thrown all away?

Though each must decide on what he should do,
It's well to put Christ first and best,
You can give God the glory for what He has done,
And choose to ignore all the rest.

You can focus attention on Christ and His Word,
Encouraging those who are near,
You can salvage the time by worshipping God,
And enjoying the folks who are dear.

Though the world may continue its usual stride,
You don't need to join in the fray,
But point folks to Jesus, the One who was born,
To wash human sins all away.

The Reason for the Season

Christmas arrives with its candles and wreaths,
Its overweight Santas, its joys, and its griefs,
With challenge of choosing each gift that is right,
While keeping the budget from taking a flight.

The bustle of shoppers that crowd every store,
The absence of hours to do any more,
The presence of people, yet feeling alone,
Can turn all expressions to faces of stone.

All of these challenges crowd out the reason
That's meant to define this wonderful season.
The Baby is left in the manger to cry
While folks by their actions His presence deny.

For the message of Christmas is somehow distorted,
When the reason Christ came is by business aborted.
And by dwelling on only His birth at this time,
We leave out His meaningful mission sublime.

Though it's well that the season brings smiles to the face,
Let us not by pursuit of its pleasures erase
The reason that Christmas brings hope every year
Is because of the Christ, whose life we revere.

Then bow at His cradle, remember His love,
And prepare in your life to embrace Him above.
Forget all the trappings for they don't compare
With the Babe in the manger who showed us His care.

The Week before Christmas

'Twas the week before Christmas and all through the town,
Much hustling and bustling was sure to be found.
The stores were all crowded with shoppers galore,
Who eagerly combed through the aisles of the store.

The clerks could be said to be mostly uptight,
Breathing sighs of relief when the doors closed at night.
The mothers looked harried; the children, wide-eyed,
While eager for all the things mothers denied.

While taking in all the confusion and sights,
I spotted a baby that brought me delight.
Amid the confusion of barter and trade,
She seemed unaffected by noise that was made.

As my eyes caught her own, she returned a sweet smile,
Contented and happy, she gazed for a while.
In that busy moment, through all of the din,
A moment of peace seemed to settle within.

One smile from the face of this innocent child,
Was enough to bring joy and contentment the while.
She seemed the fulfillment of Christmas and love,
When heaven stooped low and came down from above.

Despite all the hustle and bustle and chatter,
It's well to remember the things that still matter.
For the spirit of Christmas depends not on rings,
But consists of the music that makes the heart sing.

CPSIA information can be obtained
at www.ICGtesting.com
Printed in the USA
LVHW050540281020
669972LV00019B/429